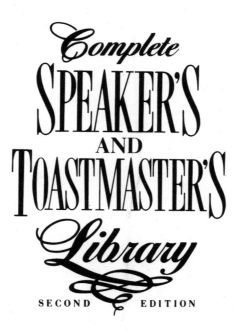

Complete
SPEAKER'S
AND
TOASTMASTER'S
Library

SECOND EDITION

Complete SPEAKER'S AND TOASTMASTER'S *Library*

SECOND EDITION

JACOB M. BRAUDE

(Glenn Van Ekeren, Revisor)

PRENTICE HALL

Paramus, New Jersey 07652

Library of Congress Catalog Card Number: 65-25224

Printed in the United States of America

10   9   8   7   6   5   4

ISBN 0-13-161597-1

9 780131 615977   90000>

ATTENTION: CORPORATIONS AND SCHOOLS

Prentice Hall books are available at quantity discounts with bulk purchase for educational, business, or sales promotional use. For information, please write to: Prentice Hall Career & Personal Development Special Sales, 240 Frisch Court, Paramus, New Jersey 07652. Please supply: title of book, ISBN number, quantity, how the book will be used, date needed.

 PRENTICE HALL
Career & Personal Development
Paramus, NJ 07652
A Simon & Schuster Company

On the World Wide Web at http://www.phdirect.com

Prentice-Hall International (UK) Limited, *London*
Prentice-Hall of Australia Pty. Limited, *Sydney*
Prentice-Hall Canada Inc., *Toronto*
Prentice-Hall Hispanoamericana, S.A., *Mexico*
Prentice-Hall of India Private Limited, *New Delhi*
Prentice-Hall of Japan, Inc., *Tokyo*
Simon & Schuster Asia Pte. Ltd., *Singapore*
Editora Prentice-Hall do Brasil, Ltda., *Rio de Janeiro*

Part 1

REMARKS OF FAMOUS PEOPLE

A

Ability

- There is something that is much more scarce, something finer far, something rarer than ability. It is the ability to recognize ability.
  —*Elbert Hubbard*

- Natural ability without education has more often raised a man to glory and virtue than education without natural ability.
  —*Cicero*

- Ability without honor is useless.
  —*Cicero*

Absence

- The same wind snuffs candles yet kindles fires; so, where absence kills a little love, it fans a great one.
  —*François de La Rochefoucauld*

Acceptance

- At the heart of personality is the need to feel a sense of being lovable without having to qualify for that acceptance.
  —*Maurice Wagner*

- Look at people; recognize them, accept them as they are, without wanting to change them.
  —*Helen Beginton*

- I have no methods; all I do is accept people as they are.
  —*Dr. Paul Tournier*

- Human beings, like plants, grow in the soil of acceptance, not in the atmosphere of rejection.
  —*John Powell, S.J.*

Acclaim

- He who seeks only for applause from without has all his happiness in another's keeping.
  —*Oliver Goldsmith*

Accommodation

- If you will please people, you must please them in their own way.
  —*Lord Chesterfield*

Accomplishment

- We do not count a man's years until he has nothing else to count.
  —*Ralph Waldo Emerson*

- Security lies in our ability to produce.
  —*Douglas MacArthur*

- So long as a man imagines that he cannot do this or that, so long is he determined not to do it; and consequently so long as it is impossible to him that he should do it.
  —*Baruch Spinoza*

- There is nothing so fatal to character as half-finished tasks.
  —*David Lloyd George*

Accuracy

- In all pointed sentences, some degree of accuracy must be sacrificed to conciseness.
  —*Dr. Samuel Johnson*

Achievement

- The greater the difficulty the more glory in surmounting it. Skillful pilots gain their reputation from storms and tempests.
  —*Epicurus*

- A man would do nothing if he waited until he could do it so well that no one would find fault with what he has done.
  —*Cardinal Newman*

- Having once decided to achieve a certain task, achieve it at all costs of tedium and distaste. The gain in self-confidence of having accomplished a tiresome labor is immense.
  —*Arnold Bennett*

- The starting point of all achievement is desire.
  —*Napoleon Hill*

- Productive achievement is a consequence and an expression of health, self-esteem, not its cause.

  —*Nathanial Brandon*

Acquisition

- That which we acquire with the most difficulty we retain the longest; as those who have earned a fortune are usually more careful of it than those who have inherited one.

  —*Charles C. Colton*

Action

- I have never heard anything about the *resolutions* of the disciples, but a great deal about the *Acts* of the Apostles.

  —*Horace Mann*

- Life is action!

  —*Oliver Wendell Holmes*

- To know just what has to be done, then do it, comprises the whole philosophy of practical life.

  —*Sir William Asner*

- Never confuse motion with action.

  —*Ernest Hemingway*

- Action expresses priorities.

  —*Charles Garfield*

- To live is not merely to breathe: it is to act; it is to make use of our organs, senses, faculties—of all those parts of ourselves which give us the feeling of existence.

  —*Jean Jacques Rousseau*

- The great end of life is not knowledge, but action. What men need is as much knowledge as they can organize for action; give them more and it may become injurious. Some men are heavy and stupid from indigested learning.

  —*Thomas Huxley*

- Nothing comes merely by thinking about it.

  —*John Wanamaker*

Actor—Actors—Acting

- They (actors) are the only honest hypocrites. Their life is a voluntary dream, a studied madness. The height of their ambition is to be beside themselves. Today kings, tomorrow beggars, it is only when they are themselves that they are nothing. Made up of mimic laughter and tears, passing from the extremes of joy or woe at the prompter's call, they wear the livery of other men's fortunes; their very thoughts are not their own.

  —*William Hazlitt*

Admiration

- There is a wide difference between admiration and love. The sublime, which is the cause of the former, always dwells on great objects and terrible; the latter on small ones and pleasing; we submit to what we admire, but we love what submits to us; in one case we are forced, in the other we are flattered, into compliance.

  —*Edmund Burke*

Adversity

- The reason why great men meet with so little pity or attachment in adversity would seem to be this. The friends of a great man were made by his fortunes, his enemies by himself, and revenge is a much more punctual paymaster than gratitude.

  —*Charles C. Colton*

- God whispers in our pleasures but shouts in our pain.

  —*C. S. Lewis*

- Need and struggle are what excite and inspire us.

  —*Willam James*

- If you faint in the day of adversity, your strength is small.

  —*King Solomon*

Advertising

- I love the man who can smile in trouble, who can gather strength from distress, and grow brave by reaction. Tis the business of little minds to shrink, but he whose heart is firm, and whose conscience approves his conduct, will pursue his principles unto death.

  —*Thomas Paine*

- Advertising may be described as the science of arresting the human intelligence long enough to get money from it.
  —*Stephen Leacock*

- Advertising is the modern substitute for argument; its function is to make the worse appear the better.
  —*George Santayana*

- The advertisements in a newspaper are more full of knowledge in respect to what is going on in a state or community than the editorial columns.
  —*Henry Ward Beecher*

- Half the money I spend on advertising is wasted; the trouble is I don't know which half.
  —*John Wanamaker*

Advice

- To accept good advice is but to increase one's ability.
  —*Johann Wolfgang von Goethe*

- When a man seeks your advice he generally wants your praise.
  —*Lord Chesterfield*

- Many receive advice, only the wise profit from it.
  —*Syrus*

Affection

- How majestic is naturalness. I have never met a man whom I really considered a great man who was not always natural and simple. Affection is inevitably the mark of one not sure of himself.
  —*Charles G. Dawes*

- My one regret in life is that I am not someone else.
  —*Woody Allen*

Affliction

- Affliction comes to all not to make us sad, but sober; not to make us sorry, but wise; not to make us despondent, but its darkness to refresh us, as the night refreshes the day; not to impoverish, but to enrich us, as the plow enriches the field; to multiply our joy, as the seed, by planting, is multiplied a thousandfold.
  —*Henry Ward Beecher*

- We can decide to let our trials crush us, or we can convert them to new forces of good.

  —Helen Keller

Age

- It is not by the gray of the hair that one knows the age of the heart.
  —Edward R. Bulwer-Lytton

- To be 70 years young is sometimes far more cheerful and hopeful than to be 40 years old.

  —Oliver Wendell Holmes

Agency

- He who does a deed by the hand of another, is the same as if he did it himself.

  —Boniface III

- I have ever held it as a maxim never to do that through another which it was impossible for me to execute myself.

  —Charles de Secondat Montesquieu

Aging

- I am not afraid of tomorrow, for I have seen yesterday and I love today.
  —William Allen White

- I've found a formula for avoiding these exaggerated fears of age: *You* take care of every day—let the calendar take care of the years.
  —Ed Wynn

- Anyone who stops learning is old, whether this happens at twenty or at eighty. Anyone who keeps on learning not only remains young but becomes constantly more valuable, regardless of physical capacity.

  —Henry Ford

- The most common cause of fear of old age is associated with the possibility of poverty.

  —Napoleon Hill

- When I was younger, I could remember anything, whether it happened or not.

  —Mark Twain

- Old age is an excellent time for outrage. My goal is to say or do at least one outrageous thing every week.

  —*Maggie Kuhn*

Agreeability

- If you wish to appear agreeable in society you must consent to be taught many things which you know already.

  — *Johann Kaspar Lavater*

Agreement

- When you say that you agree to a thing in principle you mean that you have not the slightest intention of carrying it out.

  —*Prince Otto Eduard Leopold von Bismarck-Schönhausen*

Ambition

- Most people would succeed in small things if they were not troubled by great ambitions.

  —*Henry Wadsworth Longfellow*

America—American—Americanism

- Americanism is a question of principle, of purpose, of idealism, of character; it is not a matter of birthplace or creed or line of descent.

  —*Theodore Roosevelt*

- The cornerstone of this Republic, as of all free government, is respect for and obedience to the law. Where we permit the law to be defied or evaded, whether by rich man or poor man, by black man or white, we are by just so much weakening the bonds of our civilization and increasing the chances of its overthrow, and of the substitution therefor of a system in which there shall be violent alternations of anarchy and tyranny.

  —*Theodore Roosevelt*

- Building a better you is the first step to building a better America.

  —*Zig Ziglar*

- There is nothing wrong with America that the faith, love of freedom, intelligence, and energy of her citizens cannot cure.

  —*Dwight Eisenhower*

Ancestors—Ancestry

- He who serves his country well has no need of ancestors.

  —Voltaire

Anecdote—Anecdotes

- A collection of anecdotes and maxims is the greatest of treasures for the man of the world, for he knows how to intersperse conversation with the former in fit places, and to recollect the latter on proper occasions.

  —Johann Wolfgang von Goethe

Anger

- Never forget what a man has said to you when he was angry. If he has charged you with anything, you had better look it up.

  —Harriet Ward Beecher

- Beware of him that is slow to anger; for when it is long coming, it is the stronger when it comes, and the longer kept. Abused patience turns to fury.

  —Francis Quarles

- For every minute you remain angry, you give up sixty seconds of peace of mind.

  —Emerson

- Be not hasty in your spirit to be angry . . .

  —King Solomon

- You cannot shake hands with a clenched fist.

  —Indira Ghandi

Anonymity

- No one knows where he who invented the plow was born, nor where he died; yet he has done more for humanity than the whole race of heroes who have drenched the earth with blood and whose deeds have been handed down with a precision proportionate only to the mischief they wrought.

  —Charles C. Colton

Aphorism—Aphorisms

- How many of us have been attracted to reason; first learned to think, to draw conclusions, to extract a moral from the follies of life, by some dazzling aphorism!

  —Edward R. Bulwer-Lytton

Apology

- Apologizing is a very desperate habit—one that is rarely cured. Nine times out of ten, the first thing a man's companion knows of his shortcoming is from his apology. It is mighty presumptuous on your part to suppose your small failures of so much consequence that you must talk about them.

  —Oliver Wendell Holmes

Appreciation

- People love others not for who they are but for how they make them feel.

  —Irwin Federman

Architecture

- The physician can bury his mistakes, but the architect can only advise his clients to plant vines.

  —Frank Lloyd Wright

Argument—Arguments

- It is better to debate a question without settling it than to settle it without debate.

  —Joseph Joubert

- We are not won by arguments that we can analyze but by tone and temper; by the manner which is the man himself.

  —Samuel Butler

Art

- Art does not lie in copying nature. Nature furnishes the material by means of which to express a beauty still unexpressed in nature. The Artist beholds in nature more than she herself is conscious of.

  —Henry James

Aspersion

- Be not hasty to cast off every aspersion that is cast on you. Let them alone for a while, and then, like mud on your clothes, they will rub off of themselves.

  —Dr. Nicholas Murray Butler

Associate—Associates

- We gain nothing by being with such as ourselves. We encourage one another in mediocrity. I am always longing to be with men more excellent than myself.

  —Charles Lamb

- In all societies, it is advisable to associate if possible with the highest; not that the highest are always the best, but because, if disgusted there, we can descend at any time; but if we begin with the lowest, to ascend is impossible.

  —Charles C. Colton

Association

- A puppy plays with every pup he meets, but an old dog has few associates.

  —Josh Billings

Assurance

- The best way to keep one's word is not to give it.

  —Napoleon Bonaparte

Astronomy

- Astronomy is one of the sublimest fields of human investigation. The mind that grasps its facts and principles receives something of the enlargement and grandeur belonging to the science itself. It is a quickener of devotion.

  —Horace Mann

Atheism

- A little philosophy inclineth man's mind to atheism, but depth in philosophy bringeth men's minds about to religion.

  —Francis Bacon

Attitude

- They that deny a God destroy man's nobility, for certainly man is of kin to the beasts by his body; and if he is not of kin to God by his spirit, he is a base and ignoble creature.

  —*Francis Bacon*

- No life is so hard that you can't make it easier by the way you take it.

  —*Ellen Glasgow*

- The greatest revolution of our generation is the discovery that human beings, by changing the inner attitudes of their minds, can change the outer aspects of their lives.

  —*William James*

Audience—Audiences

- It is always hard to go beyond your public. If they are satisfied with cheap performance, you will not easily arrive at better. If they know what is good, and require it, you will aspire and burn until you achieve it. But from time to time, in history, men are born a whole age too soon.

  —*Ralph Waldo Emerson*

Authorship

- A writer is dear and necessary for us only in the measure of which he reveals to us the inner workings of his very soul.

  —*Tolstoy*

- Of all that is written, I love only what a person has written with his own blood.

  —*Neitsche*

- The mind conceives with pain, but it brings forth with delight.

  —*Joseph Joubert*

- A successful author is equally in danger of the diminution of his fame, whether he continues or ceases to write.

  —*Dr. Samuel Johnson*

- Anthology construction is one of the pleasantest hobbies that a person who is not mad about golf and bridge—that is to say, a thinking person—can possibly have.

  —*Arnold Bennett*

- It is excellent discipline for an author to feel that he must say all that he has to say in the fewest possible words, or his reader is sure to skip them; and in the plainest possible words, or his reader will certainly misunderstand them. Generally, also, a downright fact may be told in a plain way; and we want downright facts at the present more than anything else.

—John Ruskin

Auto-Suggestion

- Just as you are unconsciously influenced by outside advertisement, announcement , and appeal, so you can vitally influence your life from within by auto-suggestion. The first thing each morning, and the last thing each night, suggest to yourself specific ideas that you wish to embody in your character and personality. Address such suggestions to yourself, silently or aloud, until they are deeply impressed upon your mind.

—Grenville Kleiser

Awareness

- A greater poverty than that caused by money is the poverty of unawareness. Men and women go about the world unaware of the goodness, the beauty, the glories in it. Their souls are poor. It is better to have a poor pocketbook than to suffer from a poor soul.

—Thomas Dreier

B

Banking

- It is not by augmenting the capital of the country, but by rendering a greater part of that capital active and productive than would otherwise be so, that the most judicious operations of banking can increase the industry of the country.

—Adam Smith

Bashfulness

- Mere bashfulness without merit is awkwardness.

—Joseph Addison

Beauty

- Personal beauty is a greater recommendation than any letter of introduction.

  —Aristotle

- It is better to be beautiful than to be good, but it is better to be good than to be ugly.

  —Oscar Wilde

- Though we travel the world over to find the beautiful, we must carry it with us or we find it not.

  —Ralph Waldo Emerson

Begging

- Never stand begging for that which you have the power to earn.

  —Miguel de Cervantes

- Beggars should be abolished. It annoys one to give to them, and annoys one not to give to them.

  —Friedrich Wilhelm Nietzsche

Behavior

- We often do good in order that we may do evil with impunity.

  —François de La Rochefoucauld

- Always do right. That will gratify some of the people, and astonish the rest.

  —Mark Twain

- When a man is old enough to do wrong he should be old enough to do right also.

  —Oscar Wilde

- Almost all absurdity of conduct arises from the imitation of those whom we cannot resemble.

  —Dr. Samuel Johnson

- If you treat an individual as he is, he will stay as he is; but if you treat him as if he were what he ought to be and could be, he will become what he ought to be and could be.

  —Johann Wolfgang von Goethe

- Let no man be sorry he has done good because others have done evil. If a man has acted right, he has done well, though alone; if wrong, the sanction of all mankind will not justify him.

  —*Henry Fielding*

Belief

- To believe with certainty we must begin by doubting.

  —*King Stanislas I of Poland*

- All things are possible to him who believes

  —*Jesus Christ*

- Whatever one believes to be true either is true or becomes true in one's mind.

  —*John C. Lilly*

Belittling

- Keep away from people who try to belittle your ambitions. Small people always do that, but the really great make you feel that you, too, can become great.

  —*Mark Twain*

Bias

- One can give a really unbiased opinion only about things that do not interest one, which is no doubt the reason an unbiased opinion is always valueless. The man who sees both sides of a question is a man who sees absolutely nothing.

  —*Oscar Wilde*

Bible, The

- The *Bible* among other books is as a diamond among precious stones.

  —*John Stoughton*

- The *Bible* has been the Magna Charta of the poor and of the oppressed. Down to modern times, no state has had a constitution in which the interests of the people are so largely taken into account; in which the duties, so much more than the privileges, of rulers are insisted upon, as that drawn up for Israel in Deuteronomy and Leviticus. Nowhere is the fundamental truth, that the welfare of the state, in the long run, depends upon the righteousness of the citizen, so strongly laid down. The *Bible* is the most democratic book in the world.

—*Thomas H. Huxley*

■ A thorough knowledge of the *Bible* is worth more than a college education.

—*Theodore Roosevelt*

■ It ain't those parts of the *Bible* that I can't understand that bother me, it is the parts that I do understand.

—*Mark Twain*

■ Nobody ever outgrows scripture; the Book widens and deepens with our years.

—*Charles Spurgeon*

■ The *Bible* does not provide a map for life—only a compass.

—*Haddon Robinson*

Bigness

■ The dinosaur's eloquent lesson is that if some bigness is good, an overabundance of bigness is not necessarily better. If our trend to bigness continues unrestrained, American society as we know it may be infinitely damaged. For we will move inevitably from free enterprise to socialized capitalism. And our political and personal freedoms will suffer as well. We are already moving down a road toward security rather than risk, toward belonging rather than beginning, toward adjustment rather than enterprise. The road may seem broad and pleasant . . . But what will we find at the end . . . A society that is static rather than dynamic? . . . A people who are led, rather than leading? . . . A nation grown safe and sterile and feeble at its source?

—*Eric Johnston*

Bigotry

■ The mind of the bigot is like the pupil of the eye; the more light you pour upon it, the more it will contract.

—*Oliver Wendell Holmes*

Biography

■ There is properly no history, only biography.

—*Ralph Waldo Emerson*

Boastfulness

■ To brag little—to show well—to crow gently, if in luck—to pay up, to own up, and to shut up, if beaten, are the virtues of a sporting man.

—Oliver Wendell Holmes

Book—Books

■ The oldest books are only just out to those who have not read them.

—Samuel Butler

■ Books are like a mirror. If an ass looks in, you can't expect an angel to look out.

—Arthur Schopenhauer

■ A man only learns in two ways, one by reading, and the other by association with smarter people.

—Will Rogers

■ There is no such thing as a worthless book, though there are some far worse than worthless; no book that is not worth preserving, if its existence may be tolerated; as there may be some men whom it may be proper to hang, but none who should be suffered to starve.

—Samuel T. Coleridge

Boredom

■ Life is never boring but some people choose to be bored.

—Wayne Dyer

■ The concept of boredom entails an inability to use up present moments in a personally fulfilling way.

—Wayne Dyer

■ The man who lets himself be bored is even more contemptible than the bore.

—Samuel Butler

Borrowing

■ It is a fraud to borrow what we are unable to repay.

—Publilius Syrus

Brotherhood

■ Whoever seeks to set one race against another seeks to enslave all races.

—Franklin D. Roosevelt

- We do not want the men of another color for our brothers-in-law, but we do want them for our brothers.

—*Booker T. Washington*

Bureaucracy

- Bureaucracy is a giant mechanism operated by pygmies.

—*Honoré De Balzac*

Business

- Business is a combination of war and sport.

—*André Maurois*

- Every young man would do well to remember that all successful business stands on the foundation of morality.

—*Henry Ward Beecher*

- If we devote our time disparaging the products of our business rivals, we hurt business generally, reduce confidence, and increase discontent.

—*Edward N. Hurley*

- Many persons have an idea that one cannot be in business and lead an upright life, whereas the truth is that no one succeeds in business to any great extent, who misleads or misrepresents.

—*John Wanamaker*

- Some people regard private enterprise as a predatory tiger to be shot. Others look on it as a cow they can milk. Not enough people see it as a healthy horse, pulling a sturdy wagon.

—*Winston Churchill*

C

Calamity—Calamities

- When any calamity has been suffered, the first thing to be remembered is how much has been escaped.

—*Dr. Samuel Johnson*

Capital

- The highest use of capital is not to make more money, but to make money do more for the betterment of life.

  —Henry Ford

Censorship

- One of the curious things about censorship is that no one seems to want it for himself. We want censorship to protect someone else— the young, the unstable, the suggestible, the stupid. I have never heard of anyone who wanted a film banned because otherwise he might see it and be harmed.

  —Edgar Dale

Censure

- The readiest and surest way to get rid of censure is to correct ourselves.

  —Demosthenes

Chain Reaction

- To put the world in order, we must first put the nation in order; to put the nation in order, we must put the family in order; to put the family in order, we must cultivate our personal life; and to cultivate our personal life, we must first set our hearts right.

  —Confucius

Challenges

- Accept the challenges, so that you may feel the exhilaration of victory.

  —General George S. Patton

Change

- Any change, even a change for the better, is always accompanied by drawbacks and discomforts.

  —Arnold Bennett

- Change does not necessarily assure progress, but progress implacably requires change . . . Education is essential to change, for education creates both new wants and the ability to satisfy them.

  —Henry Steele Commager

- Necessity is the author of change.

  —Tim Hansel

- Progress is a nice word, but change is its motivator and change has enemies.

  —Robert F. Kennedy

- Peak performers see the ability to manage change as a necessity in fulfilling their missions.

  —Charles Garfield

Character

- It is not what he had, or even what he does which expresses the worth of a man, but what he is.

  —Henri Frédéric Amiel

- A good character is the best tombstone. Those who loved you, and were helped by you, will remember you when forget-me-nots are withered. Carve your name on hearts, and not on marble.

  —Charles H. Spurgeon

- A man is what he is, not what men say he is. His character no man can touch. His character is what he is before his God and his Judge; and only he himself can damage that. His reputation is what men say he is. That can be damaged; but reputation is for time, character is for eternity.

  —John B. Gough

- The ultimate measure of a man is not where he stands in moments of comfort but where he stands at times of challenge and controversy.

  —Martin Luther King, Jr.

- Only what we have wrought into our character during life can we take with us.

  —Humboldt

Charity

- Be charitable before wealth makes thee covetous.

  —Sir Thomas Browne

- Proportion thy charity to the strength of thy estate, lest God proportion thy estate to the weakness of thy charity. Let the lips of the poor be the trumpet of thy gift, lest in seeking applause thou lose thy reward. Nothing is more pleasing to God than an open hand and a closed mouth.

—*Francis Quarles*

■ Joy can be real only if people look upon their life as a service, and have a definite object in life outside themselves and their personal happiness.

—*Leo Tolstoy*

■ Christian life consists of faith and charity.

—*Martin Luther*

Child—Children

■ Let your children be as so many flowers, borrowed from God. If the flowers die or wither, thank God for a summer loan of them.

—*Rev. Samuel Rutherford*

Choice

■ Our lives are a sum total of the choices we have made.

—*Dr. Wayne Dyer*

■ The history of free men is never really written by chance but by choice—their choice.

—*Dwight D. Eisenhower*

Christianity

■ If Christians would really live according to the teachings of Christ, as found in the *Bible*, all of India would be Christian today.

—*Mohandas K. Gandhi*

■ The test of Christian character should be that a man is a joy-bearing agent to the world.

—*Henry Ward Beecher*

■ Being a Christian is more than just an instantaneous conversion—it is a daily process whereby you grow to be more and more like Christ.

—*Billy Graham*

Christmas

■ Christmas would mean nothing if it were not shared with someone. It is a festival which cannot be indulged in alone. The gaudy red ribbon about the simplest gift causes that gift to take on a merit which it did not possess before; and just as a single rose may light up a room, so one word on a card, written in sincerity, may brighten the dimmest winter day.

—*Charles Hanson Towne*

Church—State

■ We know that separation of state and church is a source of strength, but the conscience of our nation does not call for separation between men of state and faith in the Supreme Being. The men who have guided the destiny of the United States have found the strength for their tasks by going to their knees. This private unity of public men and their God is an enduring source of . . . reassurance for the people of America.

—*Lyndon Baines Johnson*

Citizenship

■ The humblest citizen of all the land, when clad in the armor of a righteous cause is stronger than all the hosts of error.

— *William Jennings Bryan*

■ The first requisite of a good citizen in this republic of ours is that he shall be able and willing to pull his weight.

—*Theodore Roosevelt*

■ A citizen has a complex duty. He ought to learn to express his opinions and to make up his mind pro and con on the principal public issues. He ought never to miss the ballot box. And when he casts his vote for somebody, he should weigh that somebody in the scale of morals—including intellectual integrity.

—*Herbert Hoover*

Civilization

■ Civilization is a limitless multiplication of unnecessary necessaries.

—*Mark Twain*

■ The true test of civilization is not the census, nor the size of cities, nor the crops—no, but the kind of man the country turns out.

—*Ralph Waldo Emerson*

Common Sense

- Nothing astonishes men as much as common sense and plain dealing.

  —*Ralph Waldo Emerson*

Communication

- The way we communicate with others and with ourselves ultimately determines the quality of our lives.

  — *Anthony Robbins*

- Good communication is as stimulating as black coffee, and just as hard to sleep after.

  —*Anne Morrow Lindberg*

- The tongue is the only tool that gets sharper with use.

  —*Washington Irving*

- Half the world is composed of people who have something to say and can't and the other half who have nothing to say and keep on saying it.

  —*Robert Frost*

- When you cannot get a compliment in any other way, pay yourself one.

  —*Mark Twain*

Communism

- Only if the American people convince themselves and convince the world that they believe in liberty can we hope to meet the aggressive ideology of Communism.

  —*Robert A. Taft*

Comparison

- Comparison breeds fear, and fear breeds competition and one-upmanship.

  — *Williard & Marguerite Beecher*

- Don't find fault, find a remedy; anybody can complain.

  —*Henry Ford*

Compensation

- The world does not pay for what a person knows. But it pays for what a person does with what he knows.

  —*Laurence Lee*

Complaint—Complaints

- I think a compliment ought always to precede a complaint, where one is possible, because it softens resentment and insures for the complaint a courteous and gentle reception.

  —*Mark Twain*

Compulsion

- Anyone can do any amount of work, provided it isn't the work he is *supposed* to be doing at that moment.

  —*Robert Benchley*

Concealment

- Man is least himself when he talks in his own person. Give him a mask and he will tell the truth.

  —*Oscar Wilde*

Conceit

- I've never any pity for conceited people, because I think they carry their comfort about with them.

  —*George Eliot*

- Conceit is incompatible with understanding.

  —*Leo Tolstoy*

Concentration

- Concentration is my motto—first honesty, then industry, then concentration.

  —*Andrew Carnegie*

Conciliation

- The one sure way to conciliate a tiger is to allow oneself to be devoured.

  —*Konrad Adenauer*

- The best way to destroy your enemy is to make him your friend.
  —*Abraham Lincoln*

- Grant graciously what you cannot refuse safely and conciliate those you cannot conquer.
  —*Charles C. Colton*

Conformity

- A man must consider what a rich realm he abdicates when he becomes a conformist.
  —*Ralph Waldo Emerson*

Conscience

- Nothing is more common than for great thieves to ride in triumph when small ones are punished. But let wickedness escape as it may, as the law never fails of doing itself justice; for every guilty person is his own hangman.
  —*Seneca*

- A good conscience is a continual feast.
  —*Francis Bacon*

- If, when you look into your own heart, you find nothing wrong there, what is there to fear?
  —*Confucius*

Consequence—Consequences

- Everybody, soon or late, sits down to a banquet of consequences.
  —*Robert Louis Stevenson*

- As the dimensions of the tree are not always regulated by the size of the seed, so the consequences of things are not always proportionate to the apparent magnitude of those events that have produced them. Thus the American Revolution, from which little was expected, produced much; but the French Revolution, from which much was expected, produced little.
  —*Charles C. Colton*

Contentment

- He is richest who is content with the least, for contentment is the wealth of nature.
  —*Socrates*

- The secret of contentment is knowing how to enjoy what you have, and to be able to lose all desire for things beyond your reach.

  —*Lin Yutang*

- He is a wise man who does not grieve for the things which he has not, but rejoices for those which he has.

  —*Epictetus*

Contradiction—Contradictions

- We must not contradict, but instruct him that contradicts us; for a madman is not cured by another running mad also.

  —*Antisthenes*

Conversation

- Conversation should be pleasant without scurrility, witty without affection, free without indecency, learned without conceitedness, novel without falsehood.

  —*William Shakespeare*

Conversion

- You have not converted a man because you have silenced him.

  —*John Morley*

Cooperation

- It takes no genius to observe that a one-man band never gets very big.

  —*Charles Garfield*

- The purpose of life is to collaborate for a common cause; the problem is nobody seems to know what it is.

  —*Gerhard Gschwandtner*

- The nice thing about teamwork is that you always have others on your side.

  —*Margaret Carty*

Courage

- Courage is the capacity to conduct oneself with restraint in times of prosperity and with courage and tenacity when things do not go well.

  —*James V. Forrestal*

- Perfect courage means doing unwitnessed what we would be capable of with the world looking on.
  —*François de La Rochefoucauld*

- Courage is like love; it must have hope to nourish it.
  —*Napoleon Bonaparte*

- Courage is the power to let go of the familiar.
  —*Mary Bryant*

Courtesy

- Courtesy is the one coin you can never have too much of or be stingy with.
  —*John Wanamaker*

Covetousness

- There is no such thing as material covetousness. All covetousness is spiritual ... Any so-called material thing that you want is merely a symbol; you want it not for itself, but because it will content your spirit for the moment ... It is so with all things ... while they content the spirit they are precious, when this fails, they are worthless.
  —*Mark Twain*

Creation

- Birth and death are so closely related that one could not destroy either without destroying the other at the same time. It is extinction that makes creation possible.
  —*Samuel Butler*

Creativity

- Most people die before they are fully born. Creativeness means to be born before one dies.
  —*Eric Fromm*

- Creativity is a natural extension of our enthusiasm.
  —*Earl Nightingale*

- The possibilities of creative effort connected with the subconscious mind are stupendous and imponderable. They inspire one with awe.
  —*Napoleon Hill*

- Be brave enough to live life creatively.

—Alan Alda

Crime—Punishment

- Crime and punishment grow out of one stem. Punishment is a fruit that, unsuspected, ripens with the flower of the pleasure that concealed it.

—Ralph Waldo Emerson

Criticism

- It is much easier to be critical than to be correct.

—Benjamin Disraeli

- I learned thirty years ago that it is foolish to scold. I have enough trouble overcoming my own limitations without fretting over the fact that God has not seen fit to distribute evenly the gift of intelligence.

—John Wanamaker

- The trouble with most of us is that we would rather be ruined by praise than saved by criticism.

—Dr. Norman Vincent Peale

- I never criticize a player until they are first convinced of my unconditional confidence in their abilities.

—John Robinson

- Criticism is an indirect form of self-boasting.

—Dr. Emmet Fox

Customer Service

- A business exists to create a customer.

—Peter Drucker

- The customer perceives service in his or her own terms.

—Arch McGill

- If you're not serving the customer, you'd better be serving someone who is.

—Jan Carlzon

- Rule #1: The customer is always right. Rule #2: If the customer is wrong, see Rule #1.

—Stew Leonard

D

Death

- Death is dreadful, but in the first springtime of youth, to be snatched forcibly from the banquet to which the individual has but just sat down is peculiarly appalling.

—Sir Walter Scott

- Who knows what death is? Maybe life is nothing more than a beam of light passing slowly over our changing faces. Maybe we had a face before we were born that will live on after all our perishable faces have passed away?

—Erich Maria Remarque

- Take care of your life and the Lord will take care of your death.

—Whitefield

Decision-Making

- There is no more miserable human being than one in whom nothing is habitual but indecision.

—William James

- It does not take much strength to do things, but it requires great strength to decide what to do.

—Elbert Hubbard

- Indecision is the seedling of fear.

—Napoleon Hill

Depravity

- There is a law of neutralization of forces, which hinders bodies from sinking beyond a certain depth in the sea; but in the ocean of baseness, the deeper we get, the easier the sinking.

—James Russell Lowell

Desire—Desires

■ Nothing is enough for the man to whom enough is too little.

—Epicurus

Determination

■ In truth, people can generally make time for what they choose to do; it is not really the time but the will that is lacking.

—Sir John Lubbock

■ The fundamental qualities for good execution of a plan are, first, naturally, intelligence; then discernment and judgement, which enable one to recognize the best methods to attain it; then singleness of purpose; and, lastly, what is most essential of all, will—stubborn will.

—Ferdinand Foch

■ The difference between the impossible and the possible lies in a person's determination.

—Tommy Lasorda

■ People do not lack strength; they lack will.

—Victor Hugo

Dictatorship

■ Disregard for human beings is the first qualification of a dictator.

—Milton S. Eisenhower

Difference—Differences

■ If you pick up a starving dog and make him prosperous, he will not bite you. This is the principal difference between a dog and a man.

—Mark Twain

Difficulty

■ Difficulties mastered are opportunities won.

—Winston Churchill

■ All things are difficult before they are easy.

—John Norley

Dignity

- Dignity does not consist in possessing honors, but in deserving them.

  —Aristotle

Direction

- If a man does not know what port he is steering for, no wind is favorable to him.

  —Seneca

- The great thing in this world is not so much where we are, but in what direction we are moving.

  —Oliver Wendell Holmes

Discussion

- It is better to stir up a question without deciding it than to decide it without stirring it up.

  —Joseph Joubert

Dishonor

- A man dishonored is worse than dead.

  —Miguel de Cervantes

Dreams

- Dream lofty dreams and as you dream so shall you become; your vision is the promise of what you shall one day be.

  —James Allen

- Dreams get you into the future and add excitement to the present.

  —Bob Conklin

- In dreams begin responsibility.

  —W. B. Yeats

- We grow great by dreams.

  —Woodrow Wilson

Dress

- Those who make their dress a principal part of themselves will, in general, become of no more value than their dress.

  —William Hazlitt

Duplicity

- Nothing more completely baffles one who is full of tricks and duplicity than straightforward and simple integrity in another.

  —*Charles C. Colton*

Duty—Duties

- A duty dodged is like a debt unpaid; it is only deferred, and we must come back and settle the account at last.

  —*Joseph Fort Newton*

- If I were to try and read, much less answer, all the attacks made on me, this shop might as well be closed for any other business.

  I do the very best I know how—the very best I can, and I mean to keep doing so until the end.

  If the end brings me out all right, what is said against me won't amount to anything.

  If the end brings me out wrong, then ten angels swearing I was right would make no difference.

  —*Abraham Lincoln*

E

Eagerness

- Great eagerness in the pursuit of wealth, pleasure, or honor, cannot exist without sin.

  —*Desiderius Erasmus*

Earnestness

- Honesty is one part of eloquence. We persuade others by being in earnest ourselves.

  —*William Hazlitt*

Eating

- Choose rather to punish your appetites than be punished by them.

  —*Tyrius Maximus*

Eavesdropping

■ Take care what you say before a wall, as you cannot tell who may be behind it.

—Saadi

Eccentricity—Eccentricities

■ The amount of eccentricity in a society has generally been proportional to the amount of genius, mental vigor and moral courage it contained. That so few now dare to be eccentric marks the chief danger of the time.

—John Stuart Mill

Education

■ The roots of education are bitter, but the fruit is sweet.

—Aristotle

■ Human history becomes more and more a race between education and catastrophe.

—H. G. Wells

■ The primary purpose of education is not to teach you to earn your bread, but to make every mouthful sweeter.

—James R. Angell

■ Education is not to reform students or amuse them or to make them expert technicians. It is to unsettle their minds, widen their horizons, inflame their intellects, teach them to think straight, if possible.

—Robert M. Hutchins

■ The education of a man is never completed until he dies.

—Robert E. Lee

■ The purpose of education is to enable us to develop to the fullest that which is inside us.

—Dr. Norman Cousins

■ Education would be much more effective if its purpose was to ensure that by the time they leave school every boy and girl should know how much they do *not* know, and be imbued with a lifelong desire to know it.

—Sir William Haley

- A boy will learn more true wisdom in a public school in a year than by a private education in five. It is not from masters, but from their equals, that youth learn a knowledge of the world.
  —*Oliver Goldsmith*

Effort

- It is easier to go down a hill than up, but the view is from the top.
  —*Arnold Bennett*

Effortlessness

- Never throughout history has a man who lived a life of ease left a name worth remembering.
  —*Theodore Roosevelt*

Egotism

- If egotism means a terrific interest in one's self, egotism is absolutely essential to efficient living.
  —*Arnold Bennett*

Emotions

- When I repress my emotions, my stomach keeps score.
  —*John Powell, S. J.*

Emulation

- It is scarcely possible at once to admire and excel an author, as water rises no higher than the reservoir it falls from.
  —*Francis Bacon*

Encouragement

- The best way to cheer yourself up is to cheer someone else up.
  —*Mark Twain*

- There are two ways of exerting one's strength; one is pushing down, the other is pulling up.
  —*Booker T. Washington*

- If I can stop one heart from breaking, I shall not live in vain.
  —*Emily Dickinson*

Enemies

- Pay attention to your enemies, for they are the first to discover your mistakes.

  —Antisthenes

Enlightenment

- We can easily forgive a child who is afraid of the dark; the real tragedy of life is when men are afraid of the light.

  —Plato

Enthusiasm

- One man has enthusiasm for thirty minutes, another for thirty days, but it is the man who has it for thirty years who makes a success of his life.

  —Edward B. Butler

- Every production of genius must be the production of enthusiasm.

  —Disraeli

- If you aren't fired with enthusiasm, you will be fired . . . with enthusiasm.

  —Vince Lombardi

- No battle of any importance can be won without enthusiasm.

  —Father John O'Brian

Epigram—Epigrams

- He may justly be numbered among the benefactors of mankind, who contracts the great rules of life into short sentences, that may early be impressed on the memory, and taught by frequent recollection to occur habitually to the mind.

  —Dr. Samuel Johnson

Equanimity

- Many a happiness in life, as many a disaster, can be due to chance, but the peace within us can never be governed by chance. Call it what you may, heart, will, soul, or conscience, these words mean more or less the same thing; the spiritual riches of man. Without peace in our hearts, how can we expect peace in the world.

  —Maurice Maeterlinck

Equilibrium

■ Remember, when life's path is steep, to keep your mind even.

—*Horace*

Error—Errors

■ All wrong-doing is done in the sincere belief that it is the best thing to do.

—*Arnold Bennett*

Eulogy

■ No eulogy is due to him who simply does his duty and nothing more.

—*St. Augustine*

Evil

■ Of two evils, choose neither.

—*Charles H. Spurgeon*

■ I never wonder to see men wicked, but I often wonder to see them not ashamed.

—*Jonathan Swift*

Evolution

■ I haven't much doubt that man sprang from the monkey, but where did the monkey spring from?

—*Josh Billings*

Exactness

■ Although this may seem a paradox, all exact science is dominated by the idea of approximation. When a man tells you that he knows the exact truth about anything, you are safe in inferring that he is an *in*exact man.

—*Bertrand Russell*

Exaggeration

■ Exaggeration is a blood relation to falsehood and nearly as blamable.

—*Hosea Ballou*

Example

- People seldom improve when they have no other model but themselves to copy after.

  —Oliver Goldsmith

- Few things are harder to put up with than the annoyance of a good example.

  —Mark Twain

- I've always found that the speed of the boss is the speed of the team.

  —Lee Iacocca

Excellence

- Excellence always sells.

  —Earl Nightingale

- ... It is a wretched taste to be gratified with mediocrity when the excellent lies before us.

  —Isaac D'Israel

- Excellence is a process that should occupy all our days.

  —Ted Engstrom

- Good is not good where better is expected.

  —Thomas Fuller

Exception—Exceptions

- How glorious it is—and also how painful—to be an exception.

  —Alfred De Musset

Excessiveness

- Moderation is a fatal thing; nothing succeeds like excess.

  —Oscar Wilde

Existence

- We have come from somewhere and are going somewhere. The great architect of the universe never built a stairway that leads to nowhere.

  —Robert A. Millikan

Expectation

- Uncertainty and expectation are the joys of life. Security is an insipid thing, though the overtaking and possessing of a wish discovers the folly of the chase.

  —William Congreve

Expediency

- When virtue is lost, benevolence appears, when benevolence is lost, right conduct appears, when right conduct is lost, expedience appears. Expediency is the mere shadow of right and truth; it is the beginning of disorder.

  —Lao-Tse

Experience

- One should be careful to get out of an experience only the wisdom that is in it—and stop there; lest we be like the cat that sat down on a hot stove lid! She will never sit down on a hot stove lid again— and that's well; but also she will never sit down on a cold one anymore.

  —Mark Twain

- One thorn of experience is worth a whole wilderness of warning.

  —James Lowell

Experiment—Experimentation

- We often discover what will do by finding out what will not do; and probably he who never made a mistake never made a discovery.

  —Samuel Smiles

- It is common sense to take a method and try it. If it fails admit it frankly and try another. But above all, try something.

  —Franklin D. Roosevelt

Expert

- What's an expert? I read somewhere that the more a man knows, the more he knows he doesn't know. So I suppose one definition of an expert would be someone who doesn't admit out loud that he knows enough about a subject to know he doesn't really know much.

  —Malcolm S. Forbes

F

Fact—Facts

- When you are studying any matter or considering any philosophy, ask yourself only what are the facts and . . . the truth that the facts bear out. Never let yourself be diverted either by what you would wish to believe or by what you think would have beneficent social effects if it were believed. But look only at . . . the facts.

  —Bertrand Russell

- There is nothing as deceptive as an obvious fact.

  —Sherlock Holmes

- Neither you nor I nor Einstein nor the Supreme Court of the United States is brilliant enough to reach an intelligent decision on any problem without first getting the facts.

  —Dale Carnegie

- If the facts don't fit the theory, change the facts.

  —Albert Einstein

Faith

- Faith means belief in something concerning which doubt is theoretically possible.

  —William James

- Understanding is the reward of faith. Therefore, seek not to understand that thou mayest believe, but believe that thou mayest understand.

  —Saint Augustine

Failure

- A failure is a man who has blundered but is not able to cash in on the experience.

  —Elbert Hubbard

- Chords that were broken will vibrate once more.

  —Fanny Crosby

- No one is a failure until they blame somebody else.

  —Charlie "Tremendous" Jones

- Failures are finger posts on the road to achievement.

  —Charles F. Kettering

Fanaticism

- In the history of mankind, fanaticism has caused more harm than vice.

  —Louis Kronenberger

Fatalism

- I am prepared for the worst but hope for the best.

  —Benjamin Disraeli

Fault—Faults

- Misfortunes one can endure—they come from outside, they are accidents. But to suffer for one's own faults—ah!—there is the sting of life!

  —Oscar Wilde

Fault-Finding

- There can be no doubt that the average man blames much more than he praises. His instinct is to blame. If he is satisfied he says nothing; if he is not, he most illogically kicks up a row.

  —Arnold Bennett

Faultlessness

- We must remember not to judge any public servant by any one act, and especially should we beware of attacking the men who are merely the occasions and not the causes of disaster.

  —Theodore Roosevelt

- It is well there is no one without a fault, for he would not have a friend in the world.

  —William Hazlitt

Fear

- Fear is the sand in the machinery of life.

  —E. Stanley Jones

- They who have conquered doubt and fear have conquered failure.

  —*James Allen*

- Fears are nothing more than states of mind.

  —*Napoleon Hill*

Finance

- The way to stop financial joy-riding is to arrest the chauffeur, not the automobile.

  —*Woodrow Wilson*

- If your only goal is to become rich, you will never achieve it.

  —*John D. Rockefeller*

Flag, U.S.

- This flag means more than association and reward. It is the symbol of our national unity, our national endeavor, our national aspiration. It tells you of the struggle for independence, of union preserved, of liberty and union one and inseparable, of the sacrifice of brave men and women to whom the ideals and honors of this nation have been dearer than life.

  —*Charles Evans Hughes*

Flattery

- Flattery is never so agreeable as to our blind side; commend a fool for his wit, or a knave for his honesty, and they will receive you into their bosoms.

  —*Henry Fielding*

Fool—Fools

- Those who wish to appear wise among fools, among the wise seem foolish.

  —*Quintilian*

Forbidden

- Adam was but human—this explains it all. He did not want the apple for the apple's sake, he wanted it only because it was forbidden. The mistake was in not forbidding the serpent; then he would have eaten the serpent.

  —*Mark Twain*

Forgiveness

- He who cannot forgive others breaks the bridge over which he himself must pass.

    —*George Herbert*

- Forgiveness is the oil of relationships.

    —*Josh McDowell*

Freedom

- You can protect your liberties in this world only by protecting the other man's freedom. You can be free only if I am free.

    —*Clarence Darrow*

- He is free . . . who knows to keep in his own hands the power to decide, at each step, the course of his life and who lives in a society which does not block the exercise of that power.

    —*Salvador De Madriaga*

- Freedom means you are unobstructed in living your life as you choose. Anything less is a form of slavery.

    —*Dr. Wayne W. Dyer*

Friendship

- He that does a base thing in zeal for his friend burns the golden thread that ties their hearts together.

    —*Jeremy Taylor*

- One's friends are that part of the human race with which one can be human.

    —*George Santayana*

- Everybody needs one essential friend.

    —*Dr. William Glasser*

Frugality

- Frugality is founded on the principle that all riches have limits.

    —*Edmund Burke*

Future, The

- Only man clogs his happiness with care, destroying what *is*, with thoughts of what may be.

    —*John Dryden*

- If you do not think about the future, you cannot have one.
  —*John Galsworthy*

- The trouble with the future is that it usually arrives before we're ready for it.
  —*Arnold H. Glasow*

- Your past is important but it is not nearly as important to your present as the way you see your future.
  —*Dr. Tony Campolo*

G

Genius

- Genius does what it must, and talent does what it can.
  —*Edward Robert Bulwer-Lytton*

- Genius without religion is only a lamp on the outer gate of a palace; it may serve to cast a gleam of light on those that are without, while the inhabitant sits in darkness.
  —*Hannah More*

- The three indispensables of genius are: understanding, feeling, and perseverance; the three things that enrich genius are: contentment of mind, the cherishing of good thoughts, and the exercise of memory.
  —*Robert Southey*

- Genius means little more than the faculty of perceiving in an unhabitual way.
  —*William James*

- The only difference between a genius and one of common capacity is that the former anticipates and explores what the latter accidentally hits upon; but even the man of genius himself more frequently employs the advantages that chance presents to him; it is the lapidary who gives value to the diamond which the peasant has dug up without knowing its value.
  —*Abbé Guillaume Raynal*

Giving

- It is certainly more agreeable to have power to give than to receive.
  —*Winston Churchill*

- To give oneself is the only way of becoming oneself.
  — *Earl Nightingale*

- The essential elements of giving are power and love—activity and affection—and the consciousness of the race testifies that in the high and appropriate exercise of these is a blessedness greater than any other.
  —*Mark Hopkins*

- He that will not permit his wealth to do any good to others while he is living prevents it from doing any good to himself when he is dead; and by an egotism that is suicidal and has a double edge, cuts himself off from the truest pleasure here, and the highest happiness hereafter.
  —*Charles C. Colton*

Goal—Goals

- Aim for the top. There is plenty of room there. There are so few at the top it is almost lonely there.
  —*Samuel Insull*

- Man is a goal-seeking animal. His life only has meaning if he is reaching out and striving for his goals.
  —*Aristotle*

- Goals must never be from your ego, but problems that cry for a solution.
  —*Robert Schuller*

- Any person who selects a goal in life which can be fully achieved, has already defined his own limitations.
  —*Cavett Robert*

God—Man

- Fear God and you need not be afraid of anyone else.
  —*Woodrow Wilson*

- Whatever disunites man from God disunites man from man.
  —*Edmund Burke*

- God offers to every mind its choice between truth and repose. Take which you please—you can never have both.
  —*Ralph Waldo Emerson*

- Human nature is not so miserable as that we should be always melancholy; nor so happy as that we should be always merry. In a word, a man should not live as if there were no God in the world; nor, at the same time, as if there were no men in it.
  —*Joseph Addison*

- It makes sense that there is no sense without God.
  —*Edith Schaeffer*

- The greatest act of faith is when man understands that he is not God.
  —*Oliver Wendell Holmes*

- Blessed are the ears that hear the pulse of the divine whisperer, and give no heed to the many whisperings of the world.
  —*Thomas A. Kempis*

Good—Evil

- If you pursue good with labor, the labor passes away but the good remains; if you pursue evil with pleasure, the pleasure passes away and the evil remains.
  —*Cicero*

Good—Goodness

- Be not simply good—be good for something.
  —*Henry David Thoreau*

Good Humor

- Good humor is a tonic for mind and body. It is the best antidote for anxiety and depression. It is a business asset. It attracts and keeps friends. It lightens human burdens. It is the direct route to serenity and contentment.
  —*Grenville Kleiser*

Gossip

- Rest satisfied with doing well, and leave others to talk of you as they will.
  —*Pythagoras*

- There is so much good in the worst of us, and so much bad in the best of us, that it behooves all of us not to talk about the rest of us.
  —*Robert Louis Stevenson*

- There are two good rules which ought to be written on every heart—never to believe anything bad about anybody unless you positively know it to be true; never to tell even that unless you feel that it is absolutely necessary, and that God is listening while you tell it.
  —*Henry Van Dyke*

Government

- Government is a trust, and the officers of the government are trustees;and both the trust and the trustees are created for the benefit of the people.
  —*Henry Clay*

- Government is not a substitute for people, but simply the instrument through which they act. In the last analysis, our only freedom is the freedom to discipline ourselves.
  —*Bernard M. Baruch*

- Many people consider the things which government does for them to be social progress, but they consider the things government does for others as socialism.
  —*Earl Warren*

- Experience should teach us to be more on our guard to protect our liberties when the government's purposes are beneficent . . . The greatest dangers to liberty lurk in insidious encroachment by men of zeal, well meaning but without understanding.
  —*Louis D. Brandeis*

- The art of government is not to let men grow stale.
  —*Napoleon*

Gratitude

- To remind a man of the good turns you have done him is very much like a reproach.
  —*Demosthenes*

- When one is grateful for something too good for common thanks, writing is less unsatisfactory than speech—one does not, at least, *hear* how inadequate the words are.

  —*George Eliot*

Greatness

- To be great is to be misunderstood.

  —*Ralph Waldo Emerson*

- The man of true greatness never loses his child's heart.

  —*Mencius*

- There would be no great ones if there were no little ones.

  —*George Herbert*

- If any man seeks for greatness, let him forget greatness and ask for truth, and he will find both.

  —*Horace Mann*

- Subtract from the great man all that he owes to opportunity, all that he owes to chance, and all that he gained by the wisdom of his friends and the folly of his enemies, and the giant will often be seen to be a pygmy.

  —*Charles C. Colton*

- The man who is anybody and who does anything is surely going to be criticized, vilified, and misunderstood. This is a part of the penalty for greatness, and every great man understands it; and understands, too, that it is no proof of greatness. The final proof of greatness lies in being able to endure contumely without resentment.

  —*Elbert Hubbard*

- I believe that the first test of a truly great man is his humility. I do not mean by humility, doubt of his own power. But really great men have a curious feeling that the greatness is not in them, but through them. And they see something divine in every other man and are endlessly, foolishly, incredibly merciful.

  —*John Ruskin*

Growth

- Grow we must, if we outgrow all that love us.

  —*Oliver Wendell Holmes*

- Everybody wants to be somebody; nobody wants to grow.

  —*Johann Wolf Von Goethe*

- He who stops being better, stops being good.

  —*Oliver Cromwell*

- The strongest principle of growth lies in human choice.

  —*George Eliot*

Guilt

- It is criminal to steal a purse, daring to steal a fortune, a mark of greatness to steal a crown. The blame diminishes as the guilt increases.

  —*Friedrich von Schiller*

H

Habit—Habits

- A habit cannot be tossed out the window; it must be coaxed down the stairs a step at a time.

  —*Mark Twain*

- It seems, in fact, as though the second half of a man's life is made up of nothing but the habits he has accumulated during the first half.

  —*Feodor Mikhailovich Dostoevski*

- We first make our habits and then our habits make us.

  —*John Dryden*

Happiness

- For every minute you are angry you lose sixty seconds of happiness.

  —*Ralph Waldo Emerson*

- If one only wished to be happy, this could be easily accomplished; but we wish to be happier than other people, and this is always difficult, for we believe others to be happier than they are.

  —*Baron de La Montesquieu*

- Happiness cannot be traveled to, owned, earned, worn, or consumed. Happiness is the spiritual experience of living every minute with love, grace, and gratitude.

  —*Denis Waitley*

- Happiness lies in the joy of achievement and the thrill of creative effort.

  —*Franklin Roosevelt*

- Happiness doesn't depend on what we have, but it does depend on how we feel towards what we have. We can be happy with little and miserable with much.

  —*W. D. Hoard*

Hate—Hatred

- Hating people is like burning down your own house to get rid of a rat.

  —*Harry Emerson Fosdick*

- Those who hate you don't win unless you hate them—and then you destroy yourself.

  —*Richard M. Nixon*

Health

- Measure your health by your sympathy with morning and spring. If there is no response in you to the awakening of nature, if the prospect of an early morning walk does not banish sleep, if the warble of the first bluebird does not thrill you, know that the morning and spring of your life are past. Thus you may feel your pulse.

  —*Henry David Thoreau*

- There is this difference between the two temporal blessings—health and money; money is the most envied, but the least enjoyed; health is the most enjoyed, but the least envied; and this superiority of the latter is still more obvious when we reflect that the poorest man would not part with health for money, but that the richest would gladly part with all his money for health.

  —*Charles C. Colton*

Helpfulness

- The truest help we can render an afflicted man is not to take his burden from him, but to call out his best energy, that he may be able to bear the burden.

  —*Phillips Brooks*

Heredity

- I don't know who my grandfather was; I am much more concerned to know what his grandson will be.

  —*Abraham Lincoln*

Hero—Heroism

- There are heroes in evil as well as in good.

  —*François de La Rochefoucauld*

High-Mindedness

- Our chief usefulness to humanity rests on our combining power with high purpose. Power undirected by high purpose spells calamity; and high purpose by itself is utterly useless if the power to put it into effect is lacking.

  —*Theodore Roosevelt*

History

- History repeats itself. That's one of the things wrong with history.

  —*Clarence Darrow*

- The man who ventures to write contemporary history must expect to be attacked both for everything he has said and everything he has not said.

  —*Voltaire*

Holiness

- Those who have never tried the experiment of a holy life measure the laws of God, not by their intrinsical goodness, but by the reluctancy and opposition which they find in their hearts.

  —*Publilius Syrus*

Honesty

- It is a fine thing to be honest, but it is also very important to be right.

  —*Winston Churchill*

- Make yourself an honest man, and then you may be sure that there is one rascal less in the world.

  —Thomas Carlyle

- When in doubt, tell the truth.

  —Mark Twain

- Honesty is the first chapter of the book of wisdom.

  —Thomas Jefferson

Honor—Honors

- Dignity does not consist in possessing honors, but in deserving them.

  —Aristotle

- You can be deprived of your money, your job and your home by someone else, but remember that no one can ever take away your honor.

  —William Lyon Phelps

Human Being

- I believe in human dignity as the source of national purpose, human liberty as the source of national action, the human heart as the source of national compassion, and in the human mind as the source of our invention and our ideas.

  —John F. Kennedy

- Human kind cannot bear very much reality.

  —Thomas Sterns Elliot

Humanitarianism

- Humanitarianism consists in never sacrificing a human being to a purpose.

  —Dr. Albert Schweitzer

Humanity

- You must not lose faith in humanity. Humanity is an ocean; if a few drops of the ocean are dirty, the ocean does not become dirty.

  —Mohandas K. Gandhi

Human Nature

■ Men may change their climate, but they cannot change their nature. A man that goes out a fool cannot ride or sail himself into common sense.

—*Joseph Addison*

■ A simple experiment will distinguish two types of human nature. Gather a throng of people and pour them into a ferryboat. By the time the boat swings into the river you will find that a certain proportion have taken the trouble to climb upstairs in order to be out on deck and see what is to be seen as they cross over. The rest have settled indoors, to think what they will do upon reaching the other side, or perhaps lose themselves in apathy or tobacco smoke. But leaving out those apathetic, or addicted to a single enjoyment, we may divide all the alert passengers on the boat into two classes—those who are interested in crossing the river, and those who are merely interested in getting across.

—*Max Eastman*

Human Relations

■ Today we are faced with the preëminent fact that, if civilization is to survive, we must cultivate the science of human relationships— the ability of all peoples, of all kinds, to live together, in the same world, at peace.

—*Franklin D. Roosevelt*

Human Rights

■ God grant that not only the love of liberty but a thorough knowledge of the rights of man may pervade all the nations of the earth, so that a philosopher may set his foot anywhere on its surface and say: "This is my country!"

—*Benjamin Franklin*

■ The principle of equality of rights is quite simple. Every man can understand it, and it is by understanding his rights that he learns his duties; for where the rights of men are equal, every man must finally see the necessity of protecting the rights of others as the most effectual security of his own.

—*Thomas Paine*

Humility

■ Humility, like darkness, reveals the heavenly lights.
—*Henry David Thoreau*

■ Humility is like underwear—essential, but indecent if it shows.
—*Helen Nielsen*

■ The proud man counts his newspaper clippings—the humble man his blessings.
—*Bishop Fulton J. Sheen*

■ Don't be so humble, you're not that great.
—*Golda Meier*

Humor

■ Humor is emotional chaos remembered in tranquility.
—*James Thurber*

■ There is no reason why a joke should not be appreciated more than once. Imagine how little good music there would be if, for example, a conductor refused to play Beethoven's Fifth Symphony on the ground that his audience might have heard it before.
—*Alan Patrick Herbert*

■ Humor is laughing at what you haven't got when you ought to have it.
—*Langston Hughes*

Hypocrisy

■ The only vice which cannot be forgiven is hypocrisy. The repentance of a hypocrite is itself hypocrisy.
—*William Hazlitt*

■ When you see a man with a great deal of religion displayed in his shop window, you may depend upon it, he keeps a very small stock of it within.
—*Charles H. Spurgeon*

■ There are two sorts of hypocrites: ones that are deceived with their outward morality and external religion; and the others are those that are deceived with false discoveries and elevation; which often cry down works, and men's own righteousness, and talk much of free grace; but at the same time make righteousness of their discoveries, and of their humiliation, and exalt themselves to heaven with them.

—*Jonathan Edwards*

I

Idea—Ideas

■ Little words never hurt a big idea.

—*Howard Newton*

■ A cold in the head causes less suffering than an idea.

—*Jules Renard*

■ Money never starts an idea; it is the idea that starts the money.

—*W. J. Cameron*

■ It is useless to close the gates against ideas; they overlap them.

—*Klemens von Metternich*

■ You'll find boredom where there is the absence of a good idea.

—*Earl Nightingale*

■ Acting on a good idea is better than just having a good idea.

—*Robert Half*

■ Ideas control the world.

—*James A. Garfield*

■ All great ideas are controversial, or have been at one time.

—*George Seldes*

Ideal—Ideals

■ Show me the man you honor, and I will show you the kind of a man you are, for it shows me what your ideal of manhood is, and what kind of a man you long to be.

—*Thomas Carlyle*

■ Ideals are like stars; you will not succeed in touching them with your hands. But, like the seafaring men on the desert of waters, you choose them as your guides, and following them reach your destiny.

—*Carl Schurz*

Idleness

■ The higher men climb the longer their working day. And any young man with a streak of idleness in him may better make up his mind at the beginning that mediocrity will be his lot. Without immense, sustained effort he will not climb high. And even though fortune or chance were to lift him high, he would not stay there. For to keep at the top is harder almost than to get there. There are no office hours for leaders.

—*James Cardinal Gibbons*

Ignorance

■ Nothing is more terrible than to see ignorance in action.

—*Johann Wolfgang von Goethe*

■ The man who feels himself ignorant should, at least, be modest.

—*Dr. Samuel Johnson*

■ A man must have a certain amount of intelligent ignorance to get anywhere.

—*Charles F. Kettering*

■ Whenever you argue with another wiser than yourself in order that others may admire your wisdom, they will discover your ignorance.

—*Saadi*

Illness

■ I reckon being ill as one of the great pleasures of life, provided one is not too ill and is not obliged to work till one is better.

—*Samuel Butler*

Illusion—Illusions

■ Don't part with your illusions. When they are gone you may still exist but you have ceased to live.

—*Mark Twain*

Imagination

- Imagination is more important than knowledge.

  —Albert Einstein

Immortality

- He lives who dies to win a lasting name.

  —Henry Drummond

- A human act once set in motion flows on forever to the great account. Our deathlessness is in what we do, not in what we are.

  —George Meredith

Impatience

- In all evils which admit a remedy, impatience should be avoided, because it wastes that time and attention in complaints which, if properly applied, might remove the cause.

  —Dr. Samuel Johnson

- No good writer was ever long neglected; no great man overlooked by men equally great. Impatience is a proof of inferior strength, and a destroyer of what little there may be.

  —Walter Savage Landor

Imperfection—Imperfections

- It is only imperfection that complains of what is imperfect. The more perfect we are, the more gentle and quiet we become towards the defects of others.

  —Joseph Addison

Impossible, The

- Nothing is impossible; there are ways which lead to everything; and if we had sufficient will we should always have sufficient means.

  —François de La Rochefoucauld

Inaction

- I don't like these cold, precise, perfect people who, in order not to speak wrong, never speak at all, and in order not to do wrong, never do anything.

  —Henry Ward Beecher

Inconsiderateness

■ Ignorance and inconsideration are the two great causes of the ruin of mankind.

—*John Tillotson*

Incredulity

■ Of all the signs of a corrupt heart and a feeble head, the tendency of incredulity is the surest. Real philosophy seeks rather to solve than to deny.

—*Edward G. Bulwer-Lytton*

Indulgence

■ It is only necessary to grow old to become more indulgent. I see no fault committed that I have not committed myself.

—*Johann Wolfgang von Goethe*

Industry—Industriousness

■ In the ordinary business of life, industry can do anything which genius can do, and very many things which it cannot.

—*Harriet Ward Beecher*

Inertia

■ Life leaps like a geyser for those who drill through the rock of inertia.

—*Dr. Alexis Carrel*

Inflation

■ There are plenty of good five-cent cigars in the country. The trouble is they cost a quarter. What the country really needs is a good five-cent nickel.

—*Franklin Pierce Adams*

Influence

■ He who influences the thought of his times influences the times that follow.

—*Elbert Hubbard*

Ingenuity

- Much ingenuity with a little money is vastly more profitable and amusing than much money without ingenuity.

  —Arnold Bennett

Ingratitude

- A proud man is seldom a grateful man, for he never thinks he gets as much as he deserves.

  —Henry Ward Beecher

Injury

- The injuries we do and those we suffer are seldom weighed on the same scales.

  —Aesop

Inspiration

- Here is the secret of inspiration: Tell yourself that thousands and tens of thousands of people, not very intelligent and certainly no more intelligent than the rest of us, have mastered problems as difficult as those that now baffle you.

  —William Feather

Integrity

- Though a hundred crooked paths may conduct to a temporary success, the one plain and straight path of public and private virtue can alone lead to a pure and lasting fame and the blessings of posterity.

  —Edward Everett

Intellectual

- An intellectual is a man who takes more words than necessary to tell more than he knows.

  —Dwight D. Eisenhower

Intelligence

- Intelligence is quickness to apprehend as distinct from ability, which is capacity to act wisely on the thing apprehended.

  —Alfred North Whitehead

- Intelligence has no attachment to the opinion it has formed, but only to the truth it may contain; and, knowing that error insinuates itself under the guise of truth, through the same inlets by which truth is admitted, it is ever diffident of its attainments, and blesses the detector of errors as a benefactor and a friend.

  —*Lady Mary Wortley Montagu*

Intention—Intentions

- We know there is intention and purpose in the universe, because there is intention and purpose in us. People have said, "Where is this purpose, this intention?" I say, "It is here; it is in me; I feel it; I directly experience it, and so do you, and you need not try and look as if you didn't."

  —*George Bernard Shaw*

International Affairs

- As long as we can keep our international relations in the realm of conference rather than open conflict, we are giving truth more time to vindicate itself. And what we ourselves need is more faith in the power of truth.

  —*Ralph W. Sockman*

Internationalism

- It takes two men to make one brother.

  —*Israel Zangwill*

Intolerance

- Intolerance betrays want of faith in one's cause.

  —*Mohandas K. Gandhi*

- No human trait deserves less tolerance in everyday life, and gets less, than intolerance.

  —*Giacomo Leopardi*

- As no roads are so rough as those that have just been mended, so no sinners are so intolerant as those that have just turned saints.

  —*Charles C. Colton*

Invention—Inventions

- Accident is the name of the greatest of all inventors.

  —*Mark Twain*

- The right of an inventor to his invention is no monopoly ... in any other sense than a man's house is a monopoly.

  — *Daniel Webster*

Irrelevant—Irrelevancy

- Experience has shown, and a true philosophy will always show, that a vast, perhaps the larger portion of the truth arises from the seemingly irrelevant.

  —*Edgar Allan Poe*

J

Judge—Judges

- A good and faithful judge prefers what is right to what is expedient.

  —*Horace*

- We must remember that we have to make judges out of men, and that by being made judges their prejudices are not diminished and their intelligence is not increased.

  —*Robert G. Ingersoll*

Judgement

- You can't depend on your judgement when your imagination is out of focus.

  —*Mark Twain*

- It is because men are prone to be partial towards those they love, unjust to those they hate, servile to those above them, and either harsh or overindulgent to those below them in station, poverty or distress, that it is difficult to find anyone capable of forming a sound judgement with respect to the qualities of others.

  —*Confucius*

Jury System

- Our civilization has decided, and very justly decided, that determining the guilt or innocence of men is a thing too important to be entrusted to trained men. When it wishes for light upon that awful matter, it asks men who know no more law than I know, but who can feel the things I felt in the jury box. When it wants a library catalogued, or the solar system discovered, or any trifle of that kind, it uses up its specialists. But when it wishes anything done which is really serious, it collects twelve of the ordinary men standing around. The same thing was done, if I remember right, by the founder of Christianity.

—*G. K. Chesterton*

Justice

■ Justice is always violent to the party offending, for every man is innocent in his own eyes.

—*Daniel Defoe*

Kindness

■ Kindness in words creates confidence. Kindness in thinking creates profoundness. Kindness in giving creates love.

—*Lao-Tzu*

■ The best portion of a good man's life is in his little nameless, unremembered acts of kindness and of love.

—*Wordsworth*

Knowledge

■ True liberty can exist only when justice is equally administered to all.

—*Lord Mansfield*

■ It is more dangerous that even a guilty person should be punished without the forms of law than that he should escape.

—*Thomas Jefferson*

■ *Stare Decisis Does Not Mean Stagnation*
When (the) ghosts of the past stand in the path of justice clanking their medieval chains, the proper course for the judge is to pass through them undeterred.

—*Chief Judge Charles S. Desmond*

■ The essence of justice is mercy. Making a child suffer for wrongdoing is merciful to the child. There is no mercy in letting the child have its own will, plunging headlong to destruction with the bit in its mouth. There is no mercy to society nor to the criminal if the wrong is not repressed and the right vindicated. We injure the culprit who comes up to take his proper doom at the bar of justice, if we do not make him feel that he has done a wrong thing. We may deliver his body from the prison, but not at the expense of justice nor to his own injury.

—E. H. Chapin

■ The end of learning is to know God, and out of that knowledge to love Him and imitate Him.

—John Milton

■ Knowledge once gained casts a faint light beyond its own immediate boundaries. There is no discovery so limited as not to illuminate something beyond itself.

—John Tyndall

■ The fear of the Lord is the beginning of knowledge, but fools despise wisdom and instruction.

—King Solomon

■ Knowledge always desires increase; it is like fire, which must first be kindled by some external agent, but which will afterwards propagate itself.

—Dr. Samuel Johnson

■ Beware of false knowledge; it is more dangerous than ignorance.
—George Bernard Shaw

■ Knowledge is only potential power.

—Napoleon Hill

L

Laughter

■ The day most wholly lost is the one on which one does not laugh.
—Nicolas Chamfort

- I am persuaded that every time a man smiles—but much so when he laughs—it adds something to this fragment of life.

  — Laurence Sterne

- If you're not allowed to laugh in heaven, I don't want to go there.

  —Martin Luther

Law—Laws

- At his best man is the noblest of all animals; separated from law and justice he is the worst.

  —Aristotle

- Life and law must be kept closely in touch, as you can't adjust life to law, you must adjust law to life. The only point in having law is to make life work. Otherwise there will be explosions.

  —Arnold Toynbee

Leader—Leadership

- A leader is someone who helps improve the lives of other people or improve the system they live under.

  —Sam Ervin

- Management is about arranging and telling. Leadership is about nurturing and enhancing.

  —Tom Peters

- The first and last task of a leader is to keep hope alive.

  —Joe Batten

- Leadership appears to be the art of getting others to want to do something you are convinced should be done.

  —Vance Packard

- Leadership must be established from the top down.

  —Sam Nunn

Learning

- There are some things which cannot be learned quickly, and time, which is all we have, must be paid heavily for their acquiring. They are the very simplest things and because it takes a man's life to know them the little that each man gets from life is very costly and the only heritage he has to leave.

  —Ernest Hemingway

- The highest activity a human being can attain is learning for understanding, because to understand is to be free.

  —*Spinoza*

- Personally, I'm always ready to learn, although I do not always like being taught.

  —*Winston Churchill*

Leisure

- The more we do, the more we can do; the busier we are, the more leisure we have.

  —*William Hazlitt*

- If we don't come apart, we *will* come apart.

  —*Vance Havener*

- The time to relax is when you don't have time for it.

  —*Sydney J. Harris*

Liberalism

- A liberal is a man too broad-minded to take his own side in a quarrel.

  —*Robert Frost*

Liberty

- Liberty lies in the hearts of men and women; when it dies there, no constitution, no law, no court can save it.

  —*Learned Hand*

- Free people remember this maxim: We may acquire liberty, but it is never recovered if it is once lost.

  —*Jean Jacques Rousseau*

- They who are in the highest places, and have the most power, have the least liberty, because they are the most observed.

  —*John Tillotson*

Lie—Lies

- The essence of lying is in deception, not in words. A lie may be told by silence, by equivocation, by the accent on a syllable, by a glance of the eyes attaching a peculiar significance to a sentence; and all these kinds of lies are worse and baser by many degrees than a lie plainly worded.

—*John Ruskin*

■ Sin has many tools, but a lie is the handle that fits them all.

—*Oliver Wendell Holmes, Jr.*

■ A lie can travel half way around the world while the truth is putting on its shoes.

—*Mark Twain*

Life

■ If life were predictable it would cease to be life, and be without flavor.

—*Eleanor Roosevelt*

■ As a rule, for no one does life drag more disagreeably than for him who tries to speed it up.

—*Jean Paul Richter*

■ Life is rather a state of embryo, a preparation for life; a man is not completely born till he has passed through death.

—*Benjamin Franklin*

■ Life is either a daring adventure or it is nothing.

—*Helen Keller*

■ Don't forget until too late that the business of life is not business but living.

—*B. C. Forbes*

Limitation—Limitations

■ Don't trust children with edge tools. Don't trust man, great God, with more power than he has, until he has learned to use that little better. What a hell should we make of the world if we could do what we would! Put a button on the foil till the young fencers have learned not to put each other's eyes out.

—*Ralph Waldo Emerson*

Lincoln, Abraham

■ The Declaration of Independence was formed by the representatives of American liberty from thirteen states . . . Now, my countrymen, if you have been taught doctrines which conflict with the great landmarks of the Declaration of Independence, if you have listened to suggestion which would take from its grandeur, and mutilate the symmetry of its proportions . . . let me entreat you to come back . . . *Do not destroy that immortal emblem of Humanity, the Declaration of Independence.*

—Campaign Speech, 1858

Listening

■ A good listener is not only popular everywhere but after a while he knows something.

—Wilson Mizner

■ Very few people would listen if they didn't know it was their turn next.

—Bob Conklin

■ Give every man thy ear, but few thy voice.

—Shakespeare

Literature

■ Literature exists so that where one man has lived finely ten thousand may afterward live finely.

—Arnold Bennett

■ The reason that fiction is more interesting than any other form of literature, to those who really like to study people, is that in fiction the author can really tell the truth without humiliating himself.

—Eleanor Roosevelt

Little Things

■ The creation of a thousand forests is in one acorn.

—Ralph Waldo Emerson

Living

■ If we cannot live so as to be happy, let us at least so live as to deserve happiness.

—Johann Gottlieb Fichte

Loss—Losses

■ It may serve as a comfort to us, in all our calamities and afflictions, that he that loses anything and gets wisdom by it is a gainer by the loss.

—*Sir Roger L'Estrange*

Love

■ Love sought is good, but given unsought is better.

—*William Shakespeare*

■ There is the same difference in a person before and after he is in love as between an unlighted lamp and one that is burning. The lamp was there and it was a good lamp, but now it sheds light, too, and that is its real function. And love makes one more calm about many things, and so one is more fit for one's work.

—*Vincent van Gogh*

■ If we want to be loved we must disclose ourselves to the other person. If we want to love someone they must permit us to know them.

—*Dr. Sidney M. Jourard*

■ Loving is the only sure road out of darkness, the only serum known that cures self-centeredness.

—*Rod McKuen*

Loyalty

■ Without loyalty, nothing can be accomplished in any sphere. The person who renders loyal service in a humble capacity will be chosen for higher responsibilities, just as the Biblical servant who multiplied the one pound given him by his master was made ruler over ten cities, whereas the servant who did not put his pound to use lost that which he had.

—*B. C. Forbes*

■ Loyalty is something you give regardless of what you get back, and in giving loyalty, you're getting more loyalty. And out of loyalty flow other great qualities.

—*Charlie "Tremendous" Jones*

M

Machine—Machines

- There will still be things that machines cannot do. They will not produce great art or great literature or great philosophy; they will not be able to discover the secret springs of happiness in the human heart; they will know nothing of love and friendship. These things have in the past been squeezed out of most lives by daily toil, but, in the future, this will be unnecessary.

  —Bertrand Russell

Mankind

- You must not lose faith in humanity. Humanity is an ocean; if a few drops of the ocean are dirty, the ocean does not become dirty.

  —Mohandas K. Gandhi

Marriage

- Marriage resembles a pair of shears, so joined that they cannot be separated; often moving in opposite directions, yet always punishing anyone who comes between them.

  —H. Norman Wright

- When two people are under the influence of the most violent, most insane, most delusive, and most transient of passions, they are required to swear that they will remain in that excited, abnormal, and exhausting condition continuously until death do them part.

  —George Bernard Shaw

Materialism

- No social system will bring us happiness, health and prosperity unless it is inspired by something greater than materialism.

  —Clement R. Attlee

- It is curious circumstance that the generality of mankind are decided materialists, though without knowing it. If, indeed, you ask any persons whether they hold the soul to be material, most of them will answer no; and many would probably give the same answer if you asked them whether it is a substance; for by material, or substantial, the common people understand something tangible.

—*Richard Whately*

Meddling

■ He that blows the coals in quarrels he has nothing to do with has no right to complain if the sparks fly in his face.

—*Benjamin Franklin*

Mediocrity

■ As it is better to excel in any single art than to arrive only at mediocrity in several, so moderate skill in several is to be preferred where one cannot attain to perfection in any.

—*Pliny the Younger*

Merit

■ Real merit of any kind cannot long be concealed, it will be discovered and nothing can depreciate it but a man exhibiting it himself. It may not always be rewarded as it ought; but it will be known.

—*Lord Chesterfield*

Method

■ Irregularity and want of method are only supportable in men of great learning or genius, who are often too full to be exact, and therefore they choose to throw down their pearls in heaps before the reader, rather than be at the pains of stringing them.

—*Joseph Addison*

Mind, The

■ Your own mind is a sacred enclosure into which nothing harmful can enter except by your permission.

—*Arnold Bennett*

■ The mind conceives with pain, but it brings forth with delight.

—*Joseph Joubert*

■ There are no limitations to the mind except those we acknowledge.

—*Napoleon Hill*

Miracle—Miracles

■ The miracles of earth are the laws of heaven.

—*Jean Paul Richter*

Mischief

■ He who has a mind to do mischief will always find a pretense.

—*Publilius Syrus*

Misfortune—Misfortunes

■ Depend upon it, if a man talks of his misfortunes, there is something in them that is not disagreeable to him; for where there is nothing but pure misery, there is never any recourse to the mention of it.

—*Dr. Samuel Johnson*

Misjudgment

■ All of my misfortunes come from having thought too well of my fellows.

—*Jean Jacques Rousseau*

Mistake—Mistakes

■ The greatest mistake you can make in life is to be continually fearing you will make one.

—*Elbert Hubbard*

■ The stream of time sweeps away errors, and leaves the truth for the inheritance of humanity.

—*Georg Brandes*

■ Whenever I make a bum decision, I go out and make another one.

—*Harry Truman*

Mob

■ A mob is a society of bodies, voluntarily bereaving themselves of reason, and traversing its work. The mob is man, voluntarily descending to the nature of the beast. Its fit hour of activity is night; its actions are insane, like its whole constitution.

—*Ralph Waldo Emerson*

Modesty, False

- The man who is ostentatious of his modesty is twin to the statue that wears a fig leaf.

—*Mark Twain*

Modification

- It is a bad plan that admits of no modification.

—*Publilius Syrus*

Money

- The lack of money is the root of all evils.

—*Mark Twain*

- When you are young you think money is the most important thing in life. When you are old, you know it is.

—*Oscar Wilde*

- Those who are of the opinion that money will do everything may reasonably be expected to do everything for money.

—*Lord Halifax*

- Money is a terrible master but an excellent servant.

—*P. T. Barnum*

- Money without brains is always dangerous.

—*Napoleon Hill*

Monotony

- Monotony is the law of nature. Look at the monotonous manner in which the sun rises . . . The monotony of necessary occupations is exhilarating and life-giving.

—*Mohandas K. Gandhi*

Mother—Child

- A man never sees all that his mother has been to him until it's too late to let her know that he sees it.

—*William Dean Howells*

Motherhood

- Let France have good mothers, and she will have good sons.

—*Napoleon Bonaparte*

Motivation—Motives

- We know nothing about motivation. All we can do is write books about it.

    —*Peter Drucker*

- God made man to go by motives, and He will not go without them, any more than a boat without steam or a balloon without gas.

    —*Henry Ward Beecher*

- If your people are headed in the wrong direction, don't motivate them.

    —*George Odiorne*

Multiplicity

- Neither should a ship rely on one small anchor, nor should life rest on a single hope.

    —*Epictetus*

Music

- Music is only love looking for words.

    —*Lawrence Durrell*

Music Appreciation

- If one hears bad music it is one's duty to drown it by one's conversation.

    —*Oscar Wilde*

N

Naïvete

- It is well for the heart to be naïve and for the mind not to be.

    —*Anatole France*

Newness

- New opinions are always suspected, and usually opposed, without any other reason but because they are not already common.

    —*John Locke*

Notoriety

■ The more you are talked about, the less powerful you are.

—Benjamin Disraeli

O

Obligation—Obligations

■ When some men discharge an obligation, you can hear the report for miles around.

—Mark Twain

Obscurity

■ It is natural to every man to wish for distinction, and the praise of those who can confer honor by their praise, in spite of all false philosophy, is sweet to every human heart; but as eminence can be but the lot of a few, patience of obscurity is a duty which we owe not more to our own happiness than to the quiet of the world at large.

—Sydney Smith

Observation

■ Unless the young man looks around for himself and uses his own powers of observation and proves the assertion to be the falsity that it is, he falls under the spell of the misguidance and succumbs to a life of drudgery.

—Edward W. Bok

Obstacle—Obstacles

■ If you find a path with no obstacles, it probably doesn't lead anywhere.

—Frank A. Clark

■ I have learned that success is to be measured not so much by the position that one has reached in life as by the obstacles which he has overcome while trying to succeed.

—Booker T. Washington

- It is not ease but effort, not facility, but difficulty, that makes men. There is, perhaps no station in life in which difficulties have not to be encountered and overcome before any decided measure of success can be achieved.

—Samuel Smiles

Offense

- Whenever anyone has offended me, I try to raise my soul so high that the offense cannot reach it.

—René Descartes

Old Age

- What makes old age hard to bear is not the failing of one's faculties, mental and physical, but the burden of one's memories.

—W. Somerset Maugham

- Old age isn't so bad when you consider the alternatives.

—Maurice Chevalier

Opera

- Whenever I go to an opera, I leave my sense and reason at the door with my half guinea, and deliver myself up to my eyes and my ears.

—Lord Chesterfield

Opinion—Opinions

- There is no greater mistake than the hasty conclusion that opinions are worthless because they are badly argued.

—Thomas Huxley

- Whenever you find yourself on the side of the majority, it's time to reform.

—Will Rogers

- Man is a gregarious animal, and much more so in his mind than in his body. He may like to go alone for a walk, but he hates to stand alone in his opinions.

—George Santayana

Opportunity

- Next to knowing when to seize an opportunity, the most important thing in life is to know when to forgo an advantage.

—Disraeli

- Great minds must be ready not only to take opportunities, but to make them.

  —*Charles C. Colton*

Opposition

- Men are not against you; they are merely for themselves.

  —*Gene Fowler*

Originality

- Many a man fails as an original thinker simply because his memory is too good.

  —*Friedrich Wilhelm Nietzsche*

P

Panic—Panics

- Panics, in some cases, have their uses; they produce as much good as hurt. Their duration is always short; the mind soon grows through them and acquires a firmer habit than before. But their peculiar advantage is that they are the touchstone of sincerity and hypocrisy, and bring things and men to light, which might otherwise have lain forever undiscovered.

  —*Thomas Paine*

Parent—Child

- If you can give your son only one gift, let it be enthusiasm.

  —*Bruce Barton*

- What's done to children, they will do to society.

  —*Karl Menninger*

- Insanity is hereditary; you can get it from your children.

  —*Sam Levenson*

Past, The

- The past, though it cannot be relived, can always be repaired.

  —*John La Farge, S.J.*

Past—Present—Future

- I have but one lamp by which my feet are guided, and that is the lamp of experience. I know of no way of judging of the future but by the past.

  —*Patrick Henry*

- The past is a bucket of ashes, so live not in your yesterdays, nor just for tomorrow, but in the here and now. Keep moving and forget the post-mortems. And remember, no one can get the jump on the future.

  —*Carl Sandburg*

- Every man's life lies within the present; for the past is spent and done with, and the future is uncertain.

  —*Marcus Aurelius Antoninus*

- Those who cannot remember the past are condemned to repeat it.

  —*George Santayana*

- Those who do remember it (the past) will find new ways to screw up.

  —*Charles Wolfe*

Patience

- Patience is not passive; on the contrary, it is active; it is concentrated strength.

  —*Edward G. Bulwer-Lytton*

- It is not necessary for all men to be great in action. The greatest and sublimest power is often simple patience.

  —*Horace Bushnell*

- Genius is eternal patience.

  —*Michaelangelo*

Patriotism

- Patriotism is easy to understand in the United States. It means looking out for yourself by looking out for your country.

  —*Calvin Coolidge*

Peace

- Peace is the first thing the angels sang. Peace is the mark of the sons of God. Peace is the nurse of love. Peace is the mother of unity. Peace is the rest of blessed souls. Peace is the dwelling place for eternity.

  —Leo the Great

- Nothing can bring you peace but yourself.

  —Ralph Waldo Emerson

Perception

- The greatest thing a human soul ever does in this world is to see something and tell what it saw in a plain way. Hundreds of people can talk for one who can think, but thousands can think for one who can see. To see clearly is poetry, prophecy and religion, all in one.

  —John Ruskin

Persecution

- Curses always recoil on the head of him who imprecates them. If you put a chain around the neck of a slave, the other end fastens itself around your own . . . Every opinion reacts on him who utters it . . . You cannot do wrong without suffering wrong . . . The exclusionist in religion does not see that he shuts the door of heaven on himself, in striving to shut out others . . .

  The history of persecution is a history of endeavors to cheat nature, to make water run uphill, to twist a rope of sand. It makes no difference whether the actors be many or one, a tyrant or a mob. A mob is a society of bodies voluntarily bereaving themselves of reason and traversing its work. The mob is man voluntarily descending to the nature of the beast. Its fit hour of activity is night. Its actions are insane like its whole constitution. It persecutes a principle; it would whip a right; it would tar and feather justice by inflicting fire and outrage upon the houses and persons of those who have these . . .

  The martyr cannot be dishonored. Every lash inflicted is a tongue of fame; every prison a more illustrious abode; every burned book or house enlightens the world; every suppressed or expunged word reverberates through the earth from side to side.

  —Ralph Waldo Emerson

Perseverance

- Great works are performed not by strength but by perseverance.
  —*Dr. Samuel Johnson*

- Perseverance and tact are the two great qualities most valuable for all men who would mount, but especially for those who have to step out of the crowd.
  —*Benjamin Disraeli*

- Our greatest weakness lies in giving up. The most certain way to succeed is always to try just one more time.
  —*Thomas Edison*

Persistence

- Nothing in the world can take the place of persistence. Talent will not; nothing is more common than the unsuccessful man with talent. Genius will not; unrewarded genius is almost a proverb. Education will not; the world is full of educated derelicts. Persistence and determination alone are omnipotent. The slogan "press on" has solved and always will solve the problems of the human race.
  —*Calvin Coolidge*

- Paralyze resistance with persistence.
  —*Woody Hayes*

- We can do anything we want if we stick to it long enough.
  —*Helen Keller*

Pessimist

- There is nothing sadder than a young pessimist.
  —*Mark Twain*

- In the long run, the pessimist may be proven right, but the optimist has a better time on the trip.
  —*Daniel Reardon*

Plan—Plans—Planning

- When schemes are laid in advance, it is surprising how often circumstances fit in with them.
  —*Sir William Osler*

Platitude

- A man who has the courage of his platitudes is always a successful man. The instructed man is ashamed to pronounce in an Orphic manner what everybody knows, and because he is silent people think he is making fun of them. They like a man who expresses their own superficial thoughts in a manner that appears to be profound. This enables them to feel that they are themselves profound.

  —Van Wyck Brooks

Pleasure

- It is within the experience of everyone that when pleasure and pain reach a certain intensity they are indistinguishable.

  —Arnold Bennett

Pliability

- Our rate of progress is such that an individual human being of ordinary length of life, will be called upon to face novel situations which find no parallel in his past. The fixed person, for the fixed duties, who, in older societies was such a godsend, in the future will be a public danger.

  —Alfred North Whitehead

Poetry

- Good poetry seems too simple and natural a thing that when we meet it we wonder that all men are not always poets. Poetry is nothing but healthy speech.

  —Henry David Thoreau

Politeness

- Among well-bred people a mutual deference is affected, contempt for others is disguised; authority concealed; attention given to each in his turn; and an easy stream of conversation maintained without vehemence, without interruption, without eagerness for victory, and without any airs of superiority.

  —David Hume

Politician—Politicians

- A politician thinks of the next election; a statesman of the next generation. A politician looks for the success of his party; a statesman for that of his country. The statesman wishes to steer, while the politician is satisfied to drift.

  —James Freeman Clarke

- A politician weakly and amiably in the right is no match for a politician tenaciously and pugnaciously in the wrong. You cannot, by tying an opinion to man's tongue, make him the representative of that opinion; and at the close of any battle for principles, his name will be found neither among the dead nor among the wounded, but among the missing.

  —Edwin Percy Whipple

Politics

- He knows very little of mankind who expects, by any facts or reasoning, to convince a determined party-man.

  —Johann Kaspar Lavater

- It is an eternal truth in the political as well as the mystical body, that "where one member suffers, all the members suffer with it."

  —Junius

- An election cannot give a country a firm sense of direction if it has two or more national parties which merely have different names but are as alike in their principles and aims as two peas in the same pod.

  —Franklin D. Roosevelt

Popularity

- Seek not the favor of the multitude; it is seldom got by honest and lawful means. But seek the testimony of few; and number not voices, but weigh them.

  —Immanuel Kant

Population

- It took mankind the whole period of recorded time until the early nineteenth century to achieve a population of *one* billion, only a century to achieve a *second* billion. It took somewhat over thirty years to raise the world population to *three* billion. At the present rate of increase, only fifteen years will be required to bring the figure to *four* billion.

—John D. Rockefeller III (1963)

Positiveness

■ Positiveness is an almost absurd foible. If you are in the right, it lessens your triumph; if in the wrong, it adds shame to your defeat.

—Laurence Sterne

Possession—Possessions

■ It is preoccupation with possessions, more than anything else, that prevents men from living freely and nobly.

—Bertrand Russell

■ Think not so much of what thou hast not, as of what thou hast; but of the things which thou hast select the best, and reflect how eagerly they would have been sought if thou hadst them not.

—Marcus Aurelius

Posterity

■ There is an old Chinese saying that each generation builds a road for the next. The road has been well built for us, and I believe it incumbent upon us, in our generation, to build our road for the next generation.

—John F. Kennedy

Potential

■ There is no meaning to life except the meaning man gives it by the unfolding of his powers.

—Erich Fromm

Poverty

■ There is a noble manner of being poor, and who does not know it will never be rich.

—Seneca

■ Nature makes us poor only when we want necessaries, but custom gives the name of poverty to the want of superfluities.

—Dr. Samuel Johnson

- It would be a considerable consolation to the poor and discontented, could they but see the means whereby the wealth they covet has been acquired, or the misery that it entails.

—*J. G. Zimmerman*

Power

- The attempt to combine wisdom and power has only rarely been successful and then only for a short while.

—*Albert Einstein*

- Power will intoxicate the best hearts, as wine the strongest heads. No man is wise enough, nor good enough to be trusted with unlimited power.

—*Charles C. Colton*

- The more you are talked about, the less powerful you are.

—*Disraeli*

- Don't trust man, great God, with more power than he has, until he has learned to use that little better.

—*Ralph Waldo Emerson*

Praise

- For the good, when praised, feel something of disgust, if to excess commended.

—*Euripides*

Prayer

- I know of no manner of speaking so offensive as that of giving praise, and closing it with an exception.

—*Sir Richard Steele*

- The meanest, most contemptible kind of praise is that which first speaks well of a man, and then qualifies it with a "but."

—*Henry Ward Beecher*

- The shame that arises from praise which we do not deserve often makes us do things we should otherwise never have attempted.

—*François de La Rochefoucauld*

- Praise, like gold and diamonds, owes its value only to its scarcity. It becomes cheap as it becomes vulgar, and will no longer raise expectation or animate enterprise.

  —*Dr. Samuel Johnson*

- A prayer in its simplest definition is merely a wish turned Godward.

  —*Phillips Brooks*

- Religion is no more possible without prayer than poetry without language, or music without atmosphere.

  —*James Martineau*

- I have been driven many times to my knees, by the overwhelming conviction that I had nowhere else to go. My own wisdom, and that of all about me seemed insufficient for that day.

  —*Abraham Lincoln*

- Prayer puts you in touch with the infinite and prepares your mind for the finite.

  —*Peter Daniel*

- Prayer doesn't change God, but changes him who prays.

  —*Kierkegaard*

Preaching

- If the truth were known, many sermons are prepared and preached with more regard for the sermon than the souls of the hearers.

  —*George F. Pentecost*

- Sinclair Lewis once said in private conversation that he could not understand why ministers presumed to deliver sermons every week at appointed hours because it was humanly impossible for inspirations to come with clock-like regularity. In the same vein, Heywood Broun, the popular columnist, declared that he might resume the habit of going to church if the preacher would be honest enough to stand up some morning and say, "Perhaps next Sunday, but not today," and then sit down.

  —*The Rev. Ralph W. Sockman*

- The minister should preach as if he felt that although the congregation own the church, and have bought the pews, they have not bought him. His soul is worth no more than any other man's, but it is all he has, and he cannot be expected to sell it for a salary. The terms are by no means equal. If a parishioner does not like the preaching, he can go elsewhere and get another pew, but the preacher cannot get another soul.

—*The Rev. E. H. Chapin*

Precedent

■ When ancient opinions and rules of life are taken away, the loss cannot possibly be estimated. From that moment we have no compass to govern us, nor can we know distinctly to what port to steer.

—*Edmund Burke*

Preëminence

■ Every man who can be a first-rate something—as every man can who is a man at all—has no right to be a fifth-rate something; for a fifth-rate something is no better than a first-rate nothing.

—*Josiah G. Holland*

Prejudice

■ There is no prejudice that the work of art does not finally overcome.

—*André Gide*

■ Whoever seeks to set one race against another seeks to enslave all races.

—*Franklin D. Roosevelt*

■ The greatest and noblest pleasure which men can have in this world is to discover new truths; and the next is to shake off old prejudices.

—*Frederick the Great*

Preparation

■ Before beginning, prepare carefully.

—*Cicero*

Present, The

■ This time is a very good one if we but know what to do with it.

—*Ralph Waldo Emerson*

■ The present has nothing to do with wishing . . . when you have the present you are perfectly content to be where you are. The richness of the present comes from its own source . . . the present is not something that someone gives to you . . . it is something that you give to yourself.

—*Spencer Johnson*

Pretension

■ To give up pretensions is as blessed a relief as to get them ratified.

—*William James*

Pride

■ To be proud and inaccessible is to be timid and weak.

—*Jean Baptiste Massillon*

■ Pride that dines on vanity, sups on contempt.

—*Benjamin Franklin*

■ Pride is a vice, which pride itself inclines every man to find in others, and to overlook in himself.

—*Dr. Samuel Johnson*

■ Pride is at the bottom of all great mistakes.

—*John Ruskin*

Problems

■ People who are only good with hammers see every problem as a nail.

—*Abraham Maslow*

■ Never underestimate your problem or your ability to deal with it.

—*Dr. Robert Schuller*

■ When I am working on a problem, I never think about beauty. I think only how to solve the problem. But when I have finished, if the solution is not beautiful, I know it is wrong.

—*Buckminster Fuller*

Procrastination

■ Procrastination is: the art of keeping up with yesterday, and avoiding today.

—*Donald Marquis*

Progress

- No great advance has ever been made in science, politics, or religion, without controversy.

  —*Lyman Beecher*

- The true law of the race is progress and development. Whenever civilization pauses in the march of conquest, it is overthrown by the barbarian.

  —*William Gilmore Simms*

- The keynote of progress, we should remember, is not merely doing away with what is bad; it is replacing the best with something better.

  —*Edward A. Filene*

Promise—Promises

- Half the promises people say were never kept, were never made.

  —*E. W. Howe*

- Every civilization rests on a set of promises . . . if the promises are broken too often, the civilization dies, no matter how rich it may be, or how mechanically clever. Hope and faith depend on the promises; if hope and faith go, everything goes.

  —*Herbert Agar*

Psychoanalysis

- Psychoanalysis is confession without absolution.

  —*G. K. Chesterton*

Public, The

- The public is wiser than the wisest critic.

  —*George Bancroft*

Public Sentiment

- In this and like communities, public sentiment is everything. With public sentiment nothing can fail; without it nothing can succeed; consequently he who moulds public sentiment goes deeper than he who enacts statutes and decisions. He makes statutes and decisions possible or impossible to be executed.

  —*Abraham Lincoln*

Publisher—Publishing

- Learning hath gained most by those books by which printers have lost.

  —*Thomas Fuller*

Pugnacity

- Pugnacity is a form of courage, but a very bad form.

  —*Sinclair Lewis*

Punctuality

- If I have made an appointment with you, I owe you punctuality, I have no right to throw away your time, if I do my own.

  —*Richard Cecil*

- Lost wealth may be replaced by industry, lost knowledge by study, lost health by temperance or medicine; but lost time is gone forever.

  —*Samuel Smiles*

Punishment

- Even legal punishments lose all appearance of justice when too strictly inflicted on men compelled by the last extremity of distress to incur them.

  —*Junius*

Punishment, Capital

- We do not correct the man we hang; we correct others by him.

  —*Michel Eyquem De Montaigne*

- The punishment of criminals should be of use; when a man is hanged he is good for nothing.

  —*Voltaire*

Purpose

- The joy in life is to be used for a purpose. I want to be used up when I die.

  —*George Bernard Shaw*

- The whole life of man is but a point of time; let us enjoy it, therefore, while it lasts, and not spend it to no purpose.

  —*Plutarch*

Q

Question—Answer

- No question is so difficult to answer as that to which the answer is obvious.

  —*George Bernard Shaw*

Quotation—Quotations

- Why are not more gems from our great authors scattered over the country? Great books are not in everybody's reach; and though it is better to know them thoroughly than to know them only here and there, yet it is a good work to give a little to those who have not the time nor means to get more.

  —*Samuel T. Coleridge*

R

Race Relations

- Is it to be thought unreasonable that the people, in atonement for wrongs of a century, demand the vengeance of a single day?

  —*Maximilien François Marie Isidore De Robespierre*

Reading

- A man ought to read just as inclination leads him, for what he reads as a task will do him little good.

  —*Dr. Samuel Johnson*

- Some read books only with a view to find fault, while others read only to be taught; the former are like venomous spiders, extracting a poisonous quality, where the latter, like the bees, sip out a sweet and profitable juice.

  —*Sir Roger L'Estrange*

- Reading is to the mind what exercise is to the body. As by the one health is preserved, strengthened, and invigorated; by the other, virtue, which is the health of the mind, is kept alive, cherished, and confirmed.

  —*Sir Richard Steele*

Reason—Reasons—Reasoning

- To give a reason for anything is to breed a doubt of it.

  —*William Hazlitt*

- With children use force, with men reason; such is the natural order of things. The wise man requires no law.

  —*Jean Jacques Rousseau*

Reassurance

- Smile, for everyone lacks self-confidence . . . and more than any other one thing a smile reassures them.

  —*André Maurois*

Rebuke

- He who rebukes the world is rebuked by the world.

  —*Rudyard Kipling*

Receptivity

- There is dew in one flower and not in another, because one opens its cup and takes it in, while the other closes itself, and the drops run off. God rains his goodness and mercy as widespread as the dew, and if we lack them, it is because we will not open our hearts to receive them.

  —*Henry Ward Beecher*

Recognition

- No person was ever honored for what he received. Honor has been the reward for what he gave.

  —*Calvin Coolidge*

Recompense

- There never was a person that did anything worth doing who did not really receive more than he gave.

  —*Henry Ward Beecher*

Relationships

- It is better to live in peace than in bitterness and strife.

  —*Confucius*

- A relationship is a living thing. It needs and benefits from the same attention to detail that an artist lavishes on his art.

  —*David Viscott*

- What is unpleasant to thyself, that do not unto your neighbor. This is the whole law, all else is exposition.

  —*Hillel*

- There is no joy except in human relationships.

  —*Antoine de Saint-Exupery*

Relativity

- When a man sits with a pretty girl for an hour, it seems like a minute. But let him sit on a hot stove for a minute—and it's longer than any hour. That's relativity.

  —*Albert Einstein*

Religion

- Educate men without religion, and you make them but clever devils.

  —*Duke of Wellington*

- Even the momentary expansion of the soul in laughter is, to however slight an extent, a religious exercise ... Whenever an impulse from the world strikes against the organism, and the result is not discomfort or pain ... but a joyous expansion or aspiration of the whole soul—there is religion. It is the infinite for which we hunger, and we ride gladly on every little wave that promises to bear us towards it.

  —*Havelock Ellis*

Repayment

- Many times a day I realize how much my own life is built upon the labors of my fellowmen, and how earnestly I must exert myself in order to give in return as much as I have received.

  —*Albert Einstein*

Repentance

■ True repentance is to cease from sin.

—*St. Ambrose*

Reproach

■ Before thou reprehend another, take heed thou are not culpable in what thou goest about to reprehend. He that cleanses a blot with blotted fingers makes a greater blur.

—*Francis Quarles*

Reputation

■ It is difficult to make a reputation, but it is even more difficult seriously to mar a reputation once properly made—so faithful is the public.

—*Arnold Bennett*

Respect

■ To be capable of respect is almost as rare as to be worthy of it.

—*Joseph Joubert*

Responsibility

■ The price of greatness is responsibility.

—*Winston Churchill*

Restraint

■ Half the failures in life arise from pulling in one's horse as he is leaping.

—*J. C. and A. W. Hare*

Revenge

■ Nothing is more costly, nothing is more sterile, than vengeance.

—*Winston Churchill*

Reverence

■ Reverence is the chief joy and power of life—reverence for that which is pure and bright in youth; for what is true and tried in age; for all that is gracious among the living, great among the dead, —and marvelous in the powers that cannot die.

—*John Ruskin*

Ridicule

- It is easy for a man who sits idle at home, and has nobody to please but himself, to ridicule or censure the common practices of mankind.

—*Dr. Samuel Johnson*

Risk—Risks

- Far better it is to dare mighty things, to win glorious triumphs, even though checkered by failure, than to take rank with those poor spirits who neither enjoy much nor suffer much, because they live in the gray twilight that knows not victory nor defeat.

—*Theodore Roosevelt*

- It is only by risking our persons from one hour to another that we live at all.

—*William James*

- No man is worth his salt who is not ready at all times to risk his body ... to risk his well-being ... to risk his life ... in a great cause.

—*Theodore Roosevelt*

Rule—Rules

- There are two great rules of life, the one general and the other particular.

  The first is that everyone can, in the end, get what he wants, if he only tries. That is the general rule.

  The particular rule is that every individual is, more or less, an exception to the rule.

—*Samuel Butler*

S

Science

- The great tragedy of science—the slaying of a beautiful hypothesis by an ugly fact.

—*Thomas Huxley*

- Security is mostly a superstition. It does not exist in nature, nor do the children of men as a whole experience it. Avoiding danger is no safer in the long run than outright exposure. Life is either a daring adventure, or nothing.

  —Helen Keller

Self

- To know yourself you have only to set down a true statement of those that ever loved or hated you.

  —Johann Kaspar Lavater

- When a man is wrapped up in himself, he makes a pretty small package.

  —John Ruskin

Self-Aggrandizement

- Many hope that the tree will be felled who hope to gather chips by the fall.

  —Thomas Fuller

Self-Censure

- All censure of a man's self is oblique praise. It is in order to show how much he can spare.

  —Dr. Samuel Johnson

Self-Complacency

- The great menace to the life of an industry is industrial self-complacency.

  —David Sarnoff

Self-Development

- To reject one's own experience is to arrest one's development. To deny one's own experience is to put a lie into one's own life.

  —Oscar Wilde

Self-Discipline

- A man has to live with himself, and he should see to it that he always has good company.

  —Charles Evans Hughes

- Lack of discipline leads to frustration and self-loathing.

—*Marie Chapian*

Self-Discontent

- When a man is discontented with himself, it has one advantage . . . that it puts him into an excellent frame of mind for making a bargain.

—*Laurence Sterne*

Self-Disguise

- We are so much accustomed to disguise ourselves to others, that at length we disguise ourselves to ourselves.

—*François de La Rochefoucauld*

Self-Disparagement

- A man should be careful never to tell tales of himself to his own disadvantage; people may be amused, and laugh at the time, but they will be remembered and brought up against him upon some subsequent occasion.

—*Dr. Samuel Johnson*

Self-Distrust

- Silence is the safest course for any man to adopt who distrusts himself.

—*François de La Rochefoucauld*

Self-Examination

- In order to judge of the inside of others, study your own; for men in general are very much alike, and though one has one prevailing passion, and another has another, yet their operations are much the same; and whatever engages or disgusts, pleases, or offends you in the other will, *mutatis mutandis*, engage, disgust, please, or offend others in you.

—*Lord Chesterfield*

- When a man's fight begins within himself, he is worth something.

—*Browning*

Self-Expression

- Insist on yourself; never imitate. Your own gift can present every moment with the cumulative force of a whole life's cultivation; but of the adopted talent of another you have only an extemporaneous half-possession. That which each can do best, none but his Maker can teach him.

—*Ralph Waldo Emerson*

■ For better or worse, you must play your own little instrument in the orchestra of life.

—*Dale Carnegie*

Self-Improvement

■ Don't bother just to be better than your contemporaries or predecessors. Try to be better than yourself.

—*William Faulkner*

■ To become different from what we are, we must have some awareness of what we are.

—*Eric Hoffer*

■ A man's work is in danger of deteriorating when he thinks he has found the one best formula for doing it. If he thinks that, he is likely to feel that all he needs is merely to go on repeating himself . . . so long as a person is searching for better ways of doing his work he is fairly safe.

—*Eugene O'Neill*

Self-Inspection

■ Perpetual self-inspection leads to spiritual hypochondria. If a man insists on counting his pulse twenty times a day, on looking at his tongue every hour or two, on taking his temperature morning and evening, he will soon find himself in a doubtful state of bodily health. It is just so with those who are perpetually counting their spiritual pulse, taking the temperature of their feelings, weighing their human and necessarily imperfect characters against the infinite perfections placed in the other scale of the balance.

—*Oliver Wendell Holmes*

Selfishness

■ Selfishness is that detestable vice which no one will forgive in others and no one is without in himself.

—*Henry Ward Beecher*

■ Selfishness is the greatest curse of the human race.

—W. E. Gladstone

■ We can really respect a man only if he doesn't always *look out for himself.*

—Johann Wolfgang von Goethe

Self-Reform

■ He who reforms himself has done more toward reforming the public than a crowd of noisy, impotent patriots.

—Johann Kaspar Lavater

Self-Reproach

■ There is luxury in self-reproach. When we blame ourselves we feel no one else has a right to blame us.

—Oscar Wilde

Self-Restraint

■ I have learned to seek my happiness by limiting my desires, rather than in attempting to satisfy them.

—John Stuart Mill

Self-Service

■ The lesson of the tremendous days through which we are passing is that men cannot live upon the achievements of their forefathers, but must themselves renew them. . . . We cannot escape . . . the elementary facts of life—that for a people there is nothing for nothing, that what they have they must themselves make, that what they cherish they must themselves achieve, what they wish to keep they must themselves defend.

—Walter Lippmann

Sickness

■ It is in sickness that we most feel the need of that sympathy which shows how much we are dependent upon one another for our comfort, and even our necessities. Thus disease, opening our eyes to the realities of life, is an indirect blessing.

—Hosea Ballou

Simplicity

■ In character, in manners, in style, in all things, the supreme excellence is simplicity.

—*Henry Wadsworth Longfellow*

■ The noblest deeds are well enough set forth in simple language; emphasis spoils them.

—*Jean de La Bruyère*

Sin

■ No sin is small. It is a sin against an infinite God, and may have consequences immeasurable. No grain of sand is small in the mechanism of a watch.

—*Jeremy Taylor*

Single-Handedness

■ It is said that if Noah's ark had had to be built by a company, they would not have laid the keel yet; and it may be so. What is many men's business is nobody's business. The greatest things are accomplished by individual men.

—*Charles H. Spurgeon*

Slander

■ A slander is like a hornet; if you cannot kill it dead at the first blow, better not strike at it.

—*Josh Billings*

Sociability

■ The secret of success in society is a certain heartiness and sympathy. A man who is not happy in company, cannot find any word in his memory that will fit the occasion; all his information is a little impertinent. A man who is happy there, finds in every turn of the conversation occasions for the introduction of what he has to say. The favorites of society are able men, and of more spirit than wit, who have no uncomfortable egotism, but who exactly fill the hour and the company, contented and contenting.

—*Ralph Waldo Emerson*

Solemnity

■ Solemnity is a device of the body to hide the faults of the mind.
—*François de La Rochefoucauld*

Solitude

■ They are never alone who are accompanied with noble thoughts.
—*Sir Philip Sidney*

■ Eagles we see fly alone; and they are but sheep which always herd together.
—*Sir Philip Sidney*

Sorrow—Sorrows

■ Tearless grief bleeds inwardly.
—*Christian Nevell Bovee*

■ Any mind that is capable of real sorrow is capable of good.
—*Harriet Beecher Stowe*

■ Not in sorrow freely is never to open the bosom to the sweets of the sunshine.
—*William Gilmore Simms*

■ Has it ever occurred to us, when surrounded by sorrows, that they may be sent to us only for our instruction, as we darken the cages of birds when we wish to teach them to sing?
—*Jean Paul Richter*

Speech

■ Talking and eloquence are not the same; to speak, and to speak well are two things.
—*Ben Jonson*

■ Those who have few affairs to attend to are great speakers. The less men think, the more they talk.
—*Charles Secondat de Montesquieu*

■ Writing or printing is like shooting with a rifle; you may hit your reader's mind, or miss it—but talking is like playing at a mark with the pipe of an engine; if it is within reach, and you have time enough, you can't help hitting it.
—*Oliver Wendell Holmes*

- Let it never be said of you, "I thought he would never finish."

—*Dorothy Sarnoff*

Spending

- It is far more easy to acquire a fortune like a knave than to expend it like a gentleman.

—*Charles C. Colton*

Statesman—Statesmanship

- It is curious that we pay statesmen for what they say, not for what they do; and judge of them from what they do, not from what they say. Hence they have one code of maxims for profession and another for practice, and make up their consciences as the Neapolitans do their beds, with one set of furniture for show and another for use.

—*Charles C. Colton*

Steadfastness

- Be like a headland of rock on which the waves break incessantly; but it stands fast and around it the seething of the waters sink to rest.

—*Marcus Aurelius*

Straightforwardness

- My rule, in which I have always found satisfaction, is never to turn aside in public affairs through views of private interest, but to go straight forward in doing what appears to me right at the time, leaving the consequences with Providence.

—*Benjamin Franklin*

Strength

- We deceive ourselves when we fancy that only weakness needs support. Strength needs it far more. A straw or a feather sustains itself long in the air.

—*Anne Sophie Swetchine*

Stubbornness

- A stubborn mind conduces as little to wisdom or even to knowledge, as a stubborn temper to happiness.

—*Robert Southey*

Subjugation

■ So long as you keep a person down, there must be some part of you down there to keep him down.

—*Marian Anderson*

■ A state which dwarfs its men, in order that they may be more docile instruments in its hands, even for beneficial purposes, will find that with small men no great thing can really be accomplished.

—*John Stuart Mill*

Subservience

■ The relation between superiors and inferiors is like that between the wind and the grass. The grass must bend when the wind blows over it.

—*Confucius*

Subtlety

■ Subtlety may deceive you; integrity never will.

—*Oliver Cromwell*

Success

■ Success is the child of audacity.

—*Benjamin Disraeli*

■ Eighty percent of success is showing up.

—*Woody Allen*

■ Success consecrates the foulest crimes.

—*Seneca*

■ I do not like to repeat successes, I like to go on to other things.

—*Walt Disney*

■ Make your life a happy one. That is where success is possible to every man.

—*Sir Robert Stephenson Smyth Baden-Powell*

■ The penalty of success is to be bored by the people who used to snub you.

—*Lady Astor*

■ The ladder of success is never crowded at the top.

—*Napoleon Hill*

- Few things are impracticable in themselves; and it is for want of application, rather than of means, that men fail of success.
  —*François de La Rochefoucauld*

- The secret of success is to do the common duty uncommonly well.
  —*John D. Rockefeller, Jr.*

- To know a man, observe how he wins his object, rather than how he loses it; for when we fail, our pride supports us—when we succeed, it betrays us.
  —*Charles C. Colton*

- If you wish success in life, make perseverance your bosom friend, experience your wise counsellor, caution your elder brother, and hope your guardian genius.
  —*Joseph Addison*

- People are always blaming their circumstances for what they are. I don't believe in circumstances. The people who get on in this world are the people who get up and look for the circumstances they want, and if they can't find them, make them.
  —*George Bernard Shaw*

- The man who starts out with the idea of getting rich won't succeed: you must have a larger ambition. There is no mystery in business success. If you do each day's task successfully, stay faithful within the natural operations of commercial law, and keep your head clear, you will come out all right.
  —*John D. Rockefeller*

- A young man, to achieve, must first get out of his mind any notion either of the ease or rapidity of success. . . . Nothing ever just happens in this world: Everything is brought about. Success never comes to a man of its own volition: It will meet a man halfway, but it will never come to him all the way.
  —*Edward W. Bok*

Suffering

- It requires more courage to suffer than to die.
  —*Napoleon Bonaparte*

- Suffering becomes beautiful when anyone bears great calamity with cheerfulness, not through insensibility, but through greatness of mind.

  —*Aristotle*

Sufficiency

- There is not much difference, really, between the squirrel laying up nuts and the man laying up money. Like the squirrel, the man—at least at the start—is trying to provide for his basic needs. I don't know much about squirrels, but I think they know when they have enough nuts. In this way they are superior to men, who often don't know when they have enough, and frequently gamble away what they have in the empty hope of getting more.

  —*Bernard M. Baruch*

Suicide

- Suicide sometimes proceeds from cowardice, but not always; for cowardice sometimes prevents it; since as many live because they are afraid to die, as die because they are afraid to live.

  —*Charles C. Colton*

- Suicide is not to fear death, but yet to be afraid of life. It is a brave act of valor to condemn death; but where life is more terrible than death, it is then the truest valor to dare to live; and herein religion hath taught us a noble example, for all the valiant acts of Gaius Mucius Scaevola, or Codrus do not parallel or match that one of Job.

  —*Sir Thomas Browne*

Superficiality

- For each one striking at the roots of evil, a thousand hack merely at its branches.

  —*Henry David Thoreau*

Superiority

- What the superior man seeks is in himself, but what the small man seeks is in others.

  —*Confucius*

- No man can ever end with being superior who will not begin with being inferior.

  —*Sydney Smith*

- The superiority of some men is merely local. They are great because their associates are little.

  —*Dr. Samuel Johnson*

Superlative

- The purest ore is produced from the hottest furnace, and the brightest thunderbolt is elicited from the darkest storm.

  —*Charles C. Colton*

Superstition—Superstitions

- They that are against superstition oftentimes run into it of the wrong side. If I wear all colors but black, then I am superstitious in not wearing black.

  —*John Selden*

Surety—Suretyship

- Beware of suretyship for thy best friend. He that payeth another man's debt seeketh his own decay. But if thou canst not otherwise choose, rather lend thy money thyself upon good bonds, although thou borrow it; so shalt thou secure thyself, and pleasure thy friend.

  —*Lord Burleigh*

- If any friend desire thee to be his surety, give him a part of what thou hast spare; if he press thee further, he is not thy friend at all, for friendship rather chooseth harm to itself than offereth it. If thou be bound for a stranger, thou art a fool; if for a merchant, thou puttest thy estate to learn to swim.

  —*Sir Walter Raleigh*

Surplus

- A man with a surplus can control circumstances, but a man without a surplus is controlled by them, and often he has no opportunity to exercise judgment.

  —*Harvey Firestone*

Surrender

■ Never give in! Never give in! Never, Never, Never. Never—in nothing great or small, large or petty—never give in except to convictions of honor and good sense.

—*Winston Churchill*

Suspicion

■ Suspicion always haunts the guilty mind.

—*William Shakespeare*

■ Open suspecting of others comes of secretly condemning ourselves.

—*Sir Philip Sidney*

■ Suspicion is far more apt to be wrong than right; oftener unjust than just. It is no friend to virtue, and always an enemy to happiness.

—*Hosea Ballou*

■ Suspicion is not less an enemy to virtue than to happiness; he that is already corrupt is naturally suspicious, and he that becomes suspicious will quickly become corrupt.

—*Dr. Samuel Johnson*

■ Never put much confidence in such as put no confidence in others. A man prone to suspect evil is mostly looking in his neighbor for what he sees in himself. As to the pure all things are pure, even so to the impure all things are impure.

—*A. W. and J. C. Hare*

Sympathy

■ Sympathy is two hearts tugging at *one* load.

—*Charles H. Parkurst*

■ All sympathy not consistent with acknowledged virtue is but disguised selfishness.

—*Samuel T. Coleridge*

■ To rejoice in another's prosperity is to give content to your lot; to mitigate another's grief is to alleviate or dispel your own.

—*Tryon Edwards*

- A helping word to one in trouble is often like a switch on a railroad track—but one inch between wreck and smooth-rolling prosperity.
  —*Henry Ward Beecher*

- It is by sympathy we enter into the concerns of others, that we are moved as they are moved, and are never suffered to be indifferent spectators of almost anything which men can do or suffer. For sympathy may be considered as a sort of substitution, by which we are put into the place of another man, and affected in many respects as he is affected.
  —*Edmund Burke*

T

Taciturnity

- I have never been hurt by what I have not said.
  —*Calvin Coolidge*

Tact

- Tact consists in knowing how far to go too far.
  —*Jean Cocteau*

- We cannot always oblige, but we can always speak obligingly.
  —*Voltaire*

- Silence is not always tact, but it is tact that is golden—not silence.
  —*Samuel Butler*

Talent

- A great deal of talent is lost in the world for want of courage.
  —*Sydney Smith*

- Talent for talent's sake is a bauble and a show. Talent working with joy in the cause of universal truth lifts the possessor to new power as a benefactor.
  —*Ralph Waldo Emerson*

Talkativeness

- A man with great talents, but void of discretion, is like Polyphemus in the fable, strong and blind, endued with an irresistible force, which for want of sight is of no use to him.

  —*Joseph Addison*

- There are few wild beasts more to be dreaded than a talking man having nothing to say.

  —*Jonathan Swift*

- Every absurdity has a champion to defend it; for error is always talkative.

  —*Oliver Goldsmith*

- There are many who talk on from ignorance rather than from knowledge, and who find the former an inexhaustible fund of conversation.

  —*William Hazlitt*

Talking

- If you do not wish a man to do a thing, you had better get him to talk about it; for the more men talk, the more likely they are to do nothing else.

  —*Thomas Carlyle*

Target

- In the long run you hit only what you aim at. Therefore, though you should fail immediately, you had better aim at something high.

  —*Henry David Thoreau*

Taste

- Bad taste is a species of bad morals.

  —*Christian Nevell Bovee*

Taxes

- The repose of nations cannot be secure without arms, armies cannot be maintained without pay, nor can the pay be produced without taxes.

  —*Tacitus*

Teacher—Teachers

- Teachers should be held in the highest honor. They are the allies of legislators; they have agency in the prevention of crime; they aid in regulating the atmosphere, whose incessant action and pressure cause the life-blood to circulate, and to return pure and healthful to the heart of the nation.

  —Lydia Howard Sigourney

Teaching

- To sentence a man of true genius to the drudgery of a school is to put a racehorse in a mill.

  —Charles C. Colton

- The teacher gives not of his wisdom, but rather of his faith and lovingness.

  —Kahlil Gibran

- The whole art of teaching is only the art of awakening the natural curiosity of young minds for the purpose of satisfying it afterward.

  —Anatole France

- Good teaching must be slow enough so that it is not confusing, and fast enough so that it is not boring.

  —Sydney J. Harris

Tears

- Tears are nature's lotion for the eyes. The eyes see better for being washed by them.

  —Christian Nevell Bovee

- Tears are the natural penalties of pleasure. It is a law that we should pay for all that we enjoy.

  —William Gilmore Simms

- There is sacredness in tears. They are not the mark of weakness, but of power. They speak more eloquently than ten thousand tongues. They are the messengers of overwhelming grief, of deep contrition, and of unspeakable love.

  —Washington Irving

Temperance

■ Temperance is moderation in the things that are good and total abstinence from the things that are foul.

—*Frances E. Willard*

■ Temperance and labor are the two best physicians of man; labor sharpens the appetite, and temperance prevents from indulging to excess.

—*Jean Jacques Rousseau*

Temptation

■ Few men have virtue to withstand the highest bidder.

—*George Washington*

■ In so far as you approach temptation to a man, you do him an injury; and if he is overcome, you share his guilt.

—*Dr. Samuel Johnson*

■ Temptations, when we meet them at first, are as the lion that roared upon Samson; but if we overcome them, the next time we see them we shall find a nest of honey within them.

—*John Bunyan*

Tenderness

■ The prudence of the best heads is often defeated by the tenderness of the best hearts.

—*Henry Fielding*

■ When death, the great Reconciler, has come, it is never our tenderness that we repent of, but out severity.

—*George Eliot*

Theory—Theories

■ When I was research head of General Motors and wanted a problem solved, I'd place a table outside the meeting room with a sign: "Leave slide rules here." If I didn't do that, I'd find some engineer reaching for his slide rule. Then he'd be on his feet saying, "Boss, you can't do it."

—*Charles F. Kettering*

■ It is a capital mistake to theorize before one has data.

—*Sherlock Holmes*

Things

■ The man or woman who concentrates on "things" can hardly be trusted to use those "things" for the essential good of mankind. Only those who have guided the development of their spirit as well as their mind are really . . . qualified to use wisely the things that man's reason has enabled him to fashion out of nature's raw materials.

—*E. S. Fields*

Thinking

■ There's nothing either good or bad, but thinking makes it so.

—*William Shakespeare*

■ Thinking is the hardest work there is, which is the probable reason why so few engage in it.

—*Henry Ford*

■ Where all men think alike, no one thinks very much.

—*Walter Lippman*

■ The trouble with most people is that they think with their hopes or fears or wishes rather than with their minds.

—*Walter Duranty*

Thought—Thoughts

■ A man may dwell so long upon a thought that it may take him prisoner.

—*Lord Halifax*

■ We do not yet trust the unknown power of thoughts.

—*Ralph Waldo Emerson*

■ Change your thoughts and you change your world.

—*Norman Vincent Peale*

■ Those who do unlawful acts are no more sinners in the eyes of God than we who think them.

—*Elbert Hubbard*

■ He who thinks and thinks for himself, will always have a claim to thanks; it is no matter whether it be right or wrong, so as it be explicit. If it is right, it will serve as a guide to direct; if wrong, as a beacon to warn.

—*Jeremy Bentham*

- All that a man does outwardly is but the expression and completion of his inward thought. To work effectually, he must think clearly; to act nobly, he must think nobly. Intellectual force is a principal element of the soul's life, and should be proposed by every man as the principal end of his being.

—*William E. Channing*

Threat—Threats

- I consider it a mark of great prudence in a man to abstain from threats or any contemptuous expressions, for neither of these weaken the enemy, but threats make him more cautious, and the other excites his hatred, and a desire to revenge himself.

—*Niccolò Machiavelli*

Time

- Time—that black and narrow isthmus between two eternities.

—*Charles C. Colton*

- Time destroys the speculations of man, but it confirms the judgment of nature.

—*Cicero*

- Lost, yesterday, somewhere between sunrise and sunset, two golden hours, each set with sixty diamond minutes. Not reward is offered, for they are gone forever.

—*Horace Mann*

- We all sorely complain of the shortness of time, and yet have much more than we know what to do with. Our lives are either spent in doing nothing at all, or in doing nothing to the purpose, or in doing nothing that we ought to do. We are always complaining that our days are few, and acting as though there would be no end of them.

—*Seneca*

Time Management

- Everything requires time. It is the one truly universal condition. All work takes place in time and uses up time. Yet most people take for granted this unique, irreplaceable, and necessary resource. Nothing else, perhaps, distinguishes effective executives as much as their tender loving care of time.

—*Peter Drucker*

Timeliness

■ Nine-tenths of wisdom consists in being wise in time.

—*Theodore Roosevelt*

Timidity

■ Timidity is a fault for which it is dangerous to reprove persons whom we wish to correct of it.

—*François de La Rochefoucauld*

Title—Titles

■ Titles of honor are like the impressions on coins, which add no value to gold or silver, but only render brass current.

—*Laurence Sterne*

Tolerance

■ ... love is wise, hatred is foolish. In this world ... getting more and more closely interconnected, we have to learn to tolerate each other ... to put up with the fact that some people say things that we don't like. We can only live together in that way and if we are to live and not die together we must learn a kind of charity and ... tolerance ... absolutely vital to the continuance of human life on this planet.

—*Bertrand Russell*

Travel

■ All travel has its advantages. If the passenger visits better countries, he may learn to improve his own; and if fortune carries him to worse, he may learn to enjoy his own.

—*Dr. Samuel Johnson*

Trouble—Troubles

■ Trouble is only opportunity in work clothes.

—*Henry J. Kaiser*

■ If a man could have half his wishes he would double his troubles.

—*Benjamin Franklin*

- Trouble is the next best thing to enjoyment; there is no fate in the world so horrible as to have no share in either its joys or sorrows.

  —*Henry Wadsworth Longfellow*

- Never bear more than one kind of trouble at a time. Some people bear three kinds—all they have had, all they have now, and all they expect to have.

  —*Edward Everett Hale*

Trust

- It is better to suffer wrong than to do it, and happier to be sometimes cheated than not to trust.

  —*Dr. Samuel Johnson*

- Trust him little who praises all, him less who censures all, and him least who is indifferent about all.

  —*Johann Kaspar Lavater*

- Trust men and they will be true to you; treat them greatly and they will show themselves great.

  —*Ralph Waldo Emerson*

- You may be deceived if you trust too much, but you will live in torment if you do not trust enough.

  —*Dr. Frank Crane*

Truth

- Truth uttered before its time is dangerous.

  —*Mencius*

- No man has a good enough memory to be a successful liar.

  —*Abraham Lincoln*

- If one tells the truth, one is sure sooner or later to be found out.

  —*Oscar Wilde*

- The pursuit of truth shall set you free—even if you never catch up with it.

  —*Clarence Darrow*

- Truth often suffers more by the heat of its defenders than from the arguments of its opposers.

  —*William Penn*

- It is one thing to wish to have truth on our side, and another thing to wish to be on the side of truth.

  —*Richard Whately*

- No human being is constituted to know the truth, the whole truth and nothing but the truth; and even the best of men must be content with fragments, with partial glimpses, never the full fruition.

  —*Sir William Osler*

Tyranny

- He who strikes terror into others is himself in continual fear.

  —*Claudian*

- In every tyrant's heart there springs in the end this poison, that he cannot trust a friend.

  —*Aeschylus*

- There is a secret pride in every human heart that revolts at tyranny. You may order and drive an individual, but you cannot make him respect you.

  —*William Hazlitt*

- There is no week nor day nor hour when tyranny may not enter upon this country, if the people lose their roughness and spirit of defiance. Tyranny may always enter—there is no charm, no bar against it—the only bar against it is a large, resolute breed of men.

  —*Walt Whitman*

U

Understanding

- It is better to understand a little than to misunderstand a lot.

  —*Anatole France*

- He who does not understand your silence will probably not understand your words.

  —*Elbert Hubbard*

- Great minds comprehend more in a word, a look, a pressure of the hand than ordinary men in long conversations, or the most elaborate correspondence.

  —*Johann Kaspar Lavater*

- A blind man knows he cannot see, and is glad to be led, though it be by a dog; but he that is blind in his understanding, which is the worst blindness of all, believes he sees as the best, and scorns a guide.

  —*Samuel Butler*

- To understand others you should get behind their eyes and walk down their spines.

  —*Rod McKuen*

Unfaithfulness

- We always dread the sight of the person we love when we have been coquetting elsewhere.

  —*François de La Rochefoucauld*

Uniformity

- Where all think alike, no one thinks very much.

  —*Walter Lippmann*

- That which is to be most desired in America is oneness and not sameness. Sameness is the worst thing that could happen to the people of this country. To make all people the same would lower their quality, but oneness would raise it.

  —*Stephen S. Wise*

Unity

- Honest differences of views and honest debate are not disunity. They are the vital process of policy-making among free men.

  —*Herbert Hoover*

- The humanities and science are not in inherent conflict but have become separated in the twentieth century. Now their essential unity must be re-emphasized, so that twentieth century multiplicity may become twentieth century unity.

  —*Lewis Mumford*

Unreasonableness

■ The reasonable man adapts himself to the world; the unreasonable one persists in trying to adopt the world to himself. Therefore all progress depends on the unreasonable man.

—George Bernard Shaw

Unselfishness

■ Only a life lived for others is a life worthwhile.

—Albert Einstein

■ Do not be selfish. If you have something you do not want, and know someone who has no use for it, give it to that person. In this way you can be generous without expenditure of self-denial and also help another to be the same.

—Elbert Hubbard

■ Be unselfish. That is the first and final commandment for those who would be useful, and happy in their usefulness. If you think of yourself only, you cannot develop because you are choking the source of development, which is spiritual expansion through thought for others.

—Charles W. Eliot

Uprightness

■ A man should *be* upright, not be *kept* upright.

—Marcus Aurelius

V

Vacation—Vacations

■ Every now and then go away, have a little relaxation, for when you come back to your work your judgment will be surer since to remain constantly at work will cause you to lose power of judgment . . . Go some distance away because then the work appears smaller and more of it can be taken in at a glance and a lack of harmony and proportion is more readily seen.

—Leonardo da Vinci

Values

- Our value is the sum of our values.

  —*Joe Batten*

- Values provide perspective in the best of times and the worst.

  —*Charles Garfield*

- Expedients are for the hour; principles for the ages.

  —*H. W. Beecher*

Vanity

- To be vain is rather a mark of humility than pride.

  —*Jonathan Swift*

- It is our own vanity that makes the vanity of others intolerable to us.

  —*François de La Rochefoucauld*

Veracity

- An injurious truth has no merit over an injurious lie. Neither should ever be uttered. The man who speaks an injurious truth, lest his soul be not saved if he do otherwise, should reflect that that sort of soul is not strictly worth saving.

  —*Mark Twain*

Verbosity

- A man who uses a great many words to express his meaning is like a bad marksman who instead of aiming a single stone at an object takes up a handful and throws at it in hopes he may hit.

  —*Dr. Samuel Johnson*

Vice—Vices

- It is but a step from companionship to slavery when one associates with vice.

  —*Hosea Ballou*

- Many a man's vices have at first been nothing worse than good qualities run wild.

  —*Augustus Hare*

- It is very rare to find ground that produces nothing; if it is not covered with flowers, with fruit trees or grain, it produces weeds. It is the same with man; if he is not virtuous, he becomes vicious.

—*Jean de La Bruyère*

Victory—Victories

■ The secret of all victory lies in the organization of the non-obvious.
—*Oswald Spengler*

■ The most dangerous moment comes with victory.
—*Napoleon*

Violence

■ The violence done us by others is often less painful than that which we do to ourselves.
—*François de La Rochefoucauld*

Virtue

■ When men grow virtuous in their old age, they are merely making a sacrifice to God of the Devil's leavings.
—*Jonathan Swift*

■ They who disbelieve in virtue because man has never been found perfect, might as reasonably deny the sun because it is not always noon.
—*Augustus Hare*

Vision

■ When I think of vision, I have in mind the ability to see above and beyond the majority.
—*Charles Swindoll*

■ Envisioning the end is enough to put the means in motion.
—*Dorothea Brande*

■ Every man takes the limits of his own field of vision for the limits of the world.
—*Schopenhauer*

Vote—Votes—Voting

■ Vote for the man who promises least; he'll be the least disappointing.
—*Bernard M. Baruch*

No people is fully civilized where a distinction is drawn between stealing an office and stealing a purse.

—*Theodore Roosevelt*

W

War

■ I know war as few other men ... know it, and nothing to me is more revolting. I have long advocated its complete abolition, as its very destructiveness on both friend and foe has rendered it useless as a method of settling international disputes.

—*General Douglas MacArthur*

War—Peace

■ The world cannot continue to wage war like physical giants and to seek peace like intellectual pygmies.

—*Basil O'Connor*

Weakness

■ More men are guilty of treason through weakness than any studied design to betray.

—*François de La Rochefoucauld*

■ You cannot run away from a weakness. You must sometime fight it out or perish. And if that be so, why not now, and where you stand?

—*Robert Louis Stevenson*

■ The more weakness, the more falsehood; strength goes straight; every cannon ball that has in it hollows and holes goes crooked. Weaklings must lie.

—*Jean Paul Richter*

Wealth

■ Without a rich heart wealth is an ugly beggar.

—*Ralph Waldo Emerson*

■ Wealth is not his that has it, but his that enjoys it.

—*Benjamin Franklin*

- Seek not proud wealth; but such as thou mayest get justly, use soberly, distribute cheerfully, and love contentedly.

  —*Francis Bacon*

- Wealth, after all, is a relative thing, since he that has little, and wants less, is richer than he who has much, but wants more.

  —*Charles C. Colton*

- Gross and vulgar minds will always pay a higher respect to wealth than to talent; for wealth, although it be a far less efficient source of power than talent, happens to be far more intelligible.

  —*Charles C. Colton*

- What money creates, money preserves: if thy wealth decays, thy honor dies; it is but a slippery happiness which fortunes can give, and frowns can take; and not worth the owning which a night's fire can melt, or a rough sea can drown.

  —*Francis Quarles*

- The pulpit and the press have many commonplaces denouncing the thirst for wealth, but if men should take these moralists at their word, and leave off aiming to be rich, the moralists would rush to rekindle at all hazards this love of power in the people, lest civilization should be undone.

  —*Ralph Waldo Emerson*

Weather

- Sunshine is delicious, rain is refreshing, wind braces up, snow is exhilarating; there is no such thing as bad weather, only different kinds of good weather.

  —*John Ruskin*

Wisdom

- Fools learn nothing from wise men, but wise men learn much from fools.

  —*Johann Kaspar Lavater*

- Be very slow to believe that you are wiser than all others; it is a fatal but common error.

  —*Charles C. Colton*

- In seeking wisdom, thou art wise; in imagining that thou hast attained it, thou art a fool.

  —Rabbi Ben-Azai

- Knowledge dwells in heads replete with thoughts of other men; wisdom in minds attentive to their own.

  —William Cowper

- He who learns the rules of wisdom, without conforming to them in his life, is like a man who labored in his fields, but did not sow.

  —Saadi

- There is this difference between happiness and wisdom: he that thinks himself the happiest man is really so; but he that thinks himself the wisest is generally the greatest fool.

  —Francis Bacon

- The experience gathered from books, though often valuable, is but of the nature of learning; whereas, the experience gained from actual life is of the nature of wisdom; and a small store of the latter is worth vastly more than any stock of the former.

  —Samuel Smiles

Wit and Humor

- Wit is a dangerous weapon, even to the possessor, if he knows not how to use it discreetly.

  —Michel de Montaigne

- It is by vivacity and wit that man shines in company; but trite jokes and loud laughter reduce him to a buffoon.

  —Lord Chesterfield

Word—Words

- There are some who only employ words for the purpose of disguising their thoughts.

  —Voltaire

- "But" is a word that cools many a warm impulse, stifles many a kindly thought, puts a dead stop to many a brotherly deed. No one would ever love his neighbor as himself if he listened to all the "buts" that could be said.

  —Edward G. Bulwer-Lytton

Work

- Work is much more fun than fun.

  —*Noel Coward*

- Anyone can do any amount of work, provided it isn't the work he is supposed to be doing at that moment.

  —*Robert Benchley*

- The harder you work the luckier you get.

  —*Gary Player*

- It is not work that kills men; it is worry. Work is healthy; you can hardly put more upon a man than he can bear. Worry is rust upon the blade. It is not the revolution that destroys the machinery, but the friction.

  —*Henry Ward Beecher*

- We don't consider manual work as a curse, or a bitter necessity, not even as a means of making a living. We consider it as a high human function, as a basis of human life, the most dignified thing in the life of the human being, and which ought to be free, creative. Men ought to be proud of it.

  —*David Ben-Gurion*

Workmanship

- The glory of a workman, still more of a master-workman, that he does his work well, ought to be his most precious possession; like the honor of a soldier, dearer to him than life.

  —*Thomas Carlyle*

World, The

- The world is but a large prison, out of which some are daily selected for execution.

  —*Sir Walter Raleigh*

- This world presents enough problems if you believe it to be a world of law and order; do not add to them by believing it to be a world of miracles.

  —*Louis D. Brandeis*

- He who imagines he can do without the world deceives himself much; but he who fancies the world cannot do without him is still more mistaken.

  —*François de La Rochefoucauld*

Worry—Worries

- Worry affects the circulation, the heart, the glands, the whole nervous system. I have never known a man who died from over-work, but many who died from doubt.

  —*Dr. Charles H. Mayo*

- As a rule, men worry more about what they can't see than about what they can.

  —*Julius Caesar*

Worship

- The act of divine worship is the inestimable privilege of man, the only created being who bows in humility and adoration.

  —*Hosea Ballou*

Y

Youth

- Unless a tree has borne blossoms in spring, you will vainly look for fruit on it in autumn.

  —*Augustus Hare*

- The destiny of any nation at any given time depends on the opinions of its young men under five-and-twenty.

  —*Johann Wolfgang von Goethe*

- Unlike grown-ups, children have little need to deceive themselves.

  —*Goethe*

- The best rules to form a young man are, to talk little, to hear much, to reflect alone upon what has passed in company, to distrust one's opinions, and value others that deserve it.

  —*Sir William Temple*

- Use thy youth so that thou mayest have comfort to remember it when it hath forsaken thee, and not sigh and grieve at the account thereof. Use it as the spring-time which soon departeth, and wherein thou oughtest to plant and sow all provisions for a long and happy life.

—*Sir Walter Raleigh*

Z

Zeal

- The worst of madmen is a saint run mad.

—*Alexander Pope*

- To be furious in religion is to be irreligiously religious.

—*William Penn*

- Zeal without humility is like a ship without a rudder, liable to be stranded at any moment.

—*Owen Feltham*

- The zeal which begins with hypocrisy must conclude in treachery; at first it deceives, at last it betrays.

—*Francis Bacon*

- The eloquent man is he who is no eloquent speaker, but who is inwardly drunk with a certain belief.

—*Ralph Waldo Emerson*

- Zealous men are ever displaying to you the strength of their belief, while judicious men are showing you the grounds of it.

—*William Shenstone*

Part 2

BUSINESS AND PROFESSIONAL POINTMAKERS

A _____

Accord

- Peace is not God's gift to his creatures. It is our gift—to each other.
  —*Elie Wiesel*

- Fools bite one another, but wise men agree together.

- When two men in business always agree, one of them is unnecessary.
  —*William Wrigley, Jr.*

- You can always tell when a man's well-informed. His views are pretty much like your own.
  —*Louie Morris*

Accounts Payable

- One seasoned sales representative became increasingly concerned and frustrated with an overdue account. As a last ditch effort, she forwarded the following collection note: "Your business is appreciated, but enough is enough. Your account is now ten months overdue. That means we have carried you longer than your mother did. Immediate delivery is expected."

Actor—Acting

- Julius Tannen, after a long fame on the stage, came on hard times in Hollywood. For a number of years he was unable to get a job acting. His friends finally came to the rescue. A part was obtained for him; he was to play an editor in a newspaper drama. All that remained was for the producer to see him and pass on him.

  Tannen dressed carefully and, being completely bald, he wore a toupee for the occasion.

  The producer listened to his "sample," shook his head and said, "I'm sorry, I don't think you will do for the part. I've always visualized a bald-headed man as the man for the part."

Julius pulled the toupee slowly off his head. "I think I can satisfy you on that score," he beamed, "I happen to be completely bald."

The producer sat studying the polished Tannen skull and then shook his head again with the pronouncement, "I'm sorry, Mr. Tannen, I simply can't visualize you as a bald-headed man."

—*Ben Hecht*

Advancement

- There are people who spend their entire lives working with an attitude not unlike Snoopy, the cherished Peanuts cartoon pet. Snoopy sat droopy-eyed at the entrance of his dog house lamenting, "Yesterday I was a dog. Today I'm a dog. Tomorrow I'll probably still be a dog. SIGH. There's so little hope for advancement!"

- Hotel manager Robert Fredy was shocked and moved by the efforts of a young man one cold February day. Stephen Pearman approached his car at a New York City intersection to wash Fredy's windshield but he wasn't interested. Pearman leaned into the window. "Come on, mister, give me a break. I need a job," he said. Fredy, manager of the Berkely-Carteret Hotel in Asbury Park, New Jersey, handed the young man a business card and told him to stop in if he was serious. Two days later, 30-year-old Stephen Pearman appeared in the hotel lobby looking for the manager. Not only did he get a position setting up the hotel's banquet rooms but he even married a fellow employee. "I've gotten a second chance," he commented, "and took advantage of it."

Advertising

- Humorous advertising is doing the job. The consumer has so many distractions, so much to do, so much information clamoring for his attention, that off-beat advertising is about the only decent way of getting and holding his attention.

—*John Martins*

- P.T. Barnum once said that half the money he spent on promoting his circuses was wasted, but since he could never be sure which half, he continued to spend it all.

- Mouth to mouth is probably the best advertising vehicle; however, it isn't real effective in letting people know about your two-day sale.

- The perfect advertisement is the one that makes people happy they bought what it was you were advertising.

- The reader of a newspaper does not see the first insertion of an ordinary advertisement; the second insertion he sees but does not read; the third insertion he reads; the fourth insertion, he looks at the price; the fifth insertion, he speaks of it to his wife; the sixth insertion, he is ready to purchase; and the seventh insertion, he purchases.

  —*Unknown French Author*

- Wanted: a smart young graduate to act as deceptionist.

- Samson had the right idea about advertising. He took two columns and brought down the house.

- If you think advertising doesn't pay—we understand there are twenty-five mountains in Colorado higher than Pike's Peak. Can you name one?

- Robert Q. Lewis used to tell of a friend who had to delay opening his new store on 42nd Street in Manhattan.
  His "Going Out of Business" signs didn't arrive in time.

- The owner of a spotless new fish store in San Francisco is going to have to change the placard in his window. "We sell anything that swims," he boasted proudly.
  Then a customer walked in and demanded Esther Williams.

- "Why don't you advertise?"
  Town storekeeper: "No siree. I did once and it pretty near ruined me."
  "How was that?"
  "Why, people came in and bought dern near all the stuff I had."

- *Hard-boiled sales manager*: "Show me a single order that advertising ever put on our books."
  Salesperson: "I will , just as soon as you show me one load of hay that was ever put in the barn by the sun."

- Let advertisers spend the same amount of money improving their product that they do on advertising and they wouldn't have to advertise it.

  —*Will Rogers*

- *Genius*: "Can't understand why you failed in business."
  Friend: "Too much advertising."
  Genius: "What do you mean—too much advertising? You never spent a cent in your life on advertising."
  Friend: "That's true, but my competitor did."

- "Ad writing is a vicious circle," said the man who was making his living at it.
  "How do you mean?" asked his friend.
  "Well, I write the advertisement. Then I get paid for it. Then they print it and my family reads it. Then I pay for it."

- Max Schling, New York florist, ran an advertisement in *The New York Times* entirely in shorthand. A lot of businesspeople cut it out and, out of curiosity, asked their secretaries to translate it.
  The ad asked secretaries to think of Schling when the boss wanted flowers for his wife.

- "Well," said the dying businessperson, "you'd better put in a clause about my employees. To each employee who has worked for me twenty years I give and bequeath $50,000."
  "But," said the lawyer, "you haven't been in business twenty years."
  "I know it, but it's good advertising."

- "You mean to say you sold all those hats we had planned to discard?" asked the proprietor of the chapeau shoppe incredulously.
  "Yes," nodded the super sales manager, "I put a little ad in the paper stating that we had some hats too high-priced for the average person and they were all gone by noon."

- A storekeeper had for some time displayed in the window a card inscribed "Fishing Tickle."
  A customer drew the proprietor's attention to the spelling.
  "Hasn't anyone told you of it before?" the customer asked.
  "Hundreds," replied the dealer, "but whenever they drop in to tell me, they always spend something."

- A restaurant owner with plenty of advertising ideas and little money for advertising purchased the largest fish bowl he could find, filled it with water and put it in his window with a sign reading:

This bowl is filled with invisible Paraguayan goldfish.
It required two police officers to keep the pavements in front of the window cleared.

- An Irishman holidaying in New York went into a drug store and asked for a small tube of toothpaste. When the assistant passed him the tube, he noticed it was marked "Large."

   "I'd rather have a small one," said the Irishman.

   "Listen, bud," said the assistant, "in this country toothpaste comes in three sizes—Large, Giant and Super so if ya wanna small tube, ask for Large—see?"

- People expect canned salmon to be pink, and it is not easy to sell white salmon, even though an expert taster could hardly detect any difference. Some years ago, when pink salmon in the Columbia River were late in arriving, a canner successfully took his chances on selling the white. On each he placed a label: "This salmon is guaranteed not to turn pink in any climate."

- There was a time when Campbell Soup Company deliberately advertised "21 kinds of soup to choose from" and listed 22. For years, from 400 to 700 alert advertisement readers annually wrote the company calling attention to the discrepancy—which pleased the company immensely, the error having been made deliberately to make people talk about it and for the added purpose of giving the company an idea of how thoroughly the ad was read.

- Mark Twain once edited a paper in Missouri. One of his subscribers wrote in saying he had found a spider in his paper and wanted to know whether it meant good luck or bad. This is what Mark answered:

   "Old Subscriber: Finding a spider in your paper was neither good luck nor bad luck for you. The spider was merely looking over our paper to see which merchant is not advertising so that he can go to that store, spin his web across the door and lead a life of undisturbed peace ever afterward."

- Not long ago a patron of a restaurant in Chicago summoned a waiter and complained:

   "I want to know the meaning of this. Look at this piece of beef. See its size. Last evening I was served with a portion twice the size of this."

"Where did you sit?" asked the waiter.

"What has that to do with it? I believe I sat by the window."

"In that case," smiled the waiter, "the explanation is simple. We always serve customers by the windows large portions. It's good advertising for the place."

- A man lost a valuable dog and advertised in a newspaper offering $500 for it, but got no replies. He called at the office.

  "I want to see the advertising manager," he said.

  "She's out," said the office boy.

  "Well, how about her assistant?"

  "He's out too, sir."

  "Goodness! Is everybody out?"

  "Yes—they're all hunting your dog."

- William Wrigley, the chewing gum magnate, who amassed a great fortune, attributed his success to advertising. While traveling on a fast train shortly before his death, a friend asked him why he continued to spend millions of dollars on advertising.

  "Your gum is known the world over," argued the friend. "Why don't you save the millions you are spending on advertising?"

  Wrigley thought a moment and then asked, "How fast is this train going?"

  "About sixty miles an hour," replied the friend.

  "Then why doesn't the railway company remove the engine and let the train travel on its own momentum?" asked Wrigley.

- John Wanamaker's first advertising supervisor refused to tell anything but the literal truth in the ads. The buyer of neckties sent for him one day and asked him to get up an ad along these lines: "You can have these beautiful neckties for 25 cents, reduced from $1." The ad man looked at the ties, felt them, then asked, "Are they any good?"

  The buyer said, "No, they're not."

  The ad man went back to his office and wrote this ad:

  they're not as good as they look, but they're good enough—25 cents

  Wanamaker was buying cheap ties for three weeks to supply the demand.

Advice

- Anybody who asks for advice nowadays just hasn't been listening.

- A society band leader whose orchestras have played for some ten thousand weddings told the musicians:
  "Always play your best. Remember, at least one out of every five of these couples gets married again."

- Always advise a friend to do that which you are sure they are not going to do. Then if their venture fails, you will receive credit for having warned them. If it succeeds, they will be happy in the opportunity to tell you that you were dead wrong.

- Two battered old hulks of humanity were sitting together on a park bench. One of them leaned over and said to his neighbor, "I'm a man who never took advice from anybody."
  "Shake, pal," said the other, "I'm the man who followed everybody's advice."

Affluence

- True affluence is not needing anything.
  —*Gary Snyder*

Age

- If you carry your childhood with you, you never become older.
  —*Abraham Sutzkeuer*

- "Why, look here," said the retailer who was in need of a sales clerk, "aren't you the same boy who was in here a week ago?"
  "Yes, sir," said the applicant.
  "I thought so. And didn't I tell you that I wanted someone older?"
  "Yes, sir. That's why I'm back. I'm older now."

Alternative—Alternatives

- A company that manufactured soap and perfume offered a prize for the best slogan submitted for the advertising of its products. The judges easily agreed on the best slogan, but did not give it the prize. The slogan was: "If you don't use our soap, for heaven's sake use our perfume!"

America—American—Americanism

- There can be no daily democracy without daily citizenship.

  —Ralph Nader

- The typical successful American businessperson was born in the country, where they worked with great energy so they could live in the city, where they worked with even greater energy so they could live in the country!

- Definition of an American: A person drinking Brazilian coffee from an English cup, while sitting on Danish furniture after coming home in a German car from an Italian movie, who picks up a Japanese ball point pen and writes a letter to his congressperson demanding that something be done about spending the country's diminishing dollar reserves on Venezuelan oil.

- If you want your father to take care of you, that's paternalism...

  If you want your mother to take care of you, that's maternalism...

  If you want Uncle Sam to take care of you, that's Socialism...

  If you want your comrades to take care of you, that's Communism...

  But if you want to take care of yourself, that's Americanism.

- Two buckets of live crabs were side by side at a fish market, and labeled $1.50 a dozen and $2.00 a dozen. A dowager stood viewing them when suddenly a crab from the $1.50 tub climbed up with much effort and dropped into the $2.00 tub.

  "That's the sort of thing," remarked the dowager to one of her companions, "which could happen only in America."

Ancestry

- "I want a dog of which I can be proud," said Mrs. Newlyrich. "Does that one have a good pedigree?"

  "Lady," declared the kennel owner, "if he could talk, he wouldn't speak to either of us."

- A descendant of the noble Harmodius was taunting Iphicrates with his low birth.

  "The difference between us is this," Iphicrates replied, "my family begins with me, and yours ends with you."

■ Signor Marconi, inventor of wireless telegraphy, was once interviewed in Washington, and spoke in praise of American democracy.

"Over here" he said, "you respect a man for what he is himself—not for what his family is—and thus you remind one of the gardener in Bologna who helped me with my first wireless apparatus.

"As we worked together on the apparatus a young count joined us one day, and while he watched us work he boasted of his lineage.

"The gardener, after listening a long while smiled and said:

"'If you come from an ancient family, it's so much the worse for you, sir; for, as we gardeners say, the older the seed the worse the crop.'"

Antique—Antiques

■ Henny Youngman used to tell of the time he was ejected from an antique shop. "All I did," he said, "was walk in and ask 'What's new?'"

■ Outside the village of Nantucket a house had been converted into a store. At the roadside the proprietor had posted this: *We Buy Trash and Sell Antiques.*

■ *Customer:* "What! Five hundred dollars for that antique! Why, I priced it last week and you said three hundred and fifty."

Dealer: "Yes, I know; but the cost of labor and materials has gone up so!"

■ An architect was having a difficult time with a prospective home builder. "But can't you give me *some* idea," he pleaded, "of the general type of house you want to build?"

"Well—" replied the man hesitantly, "all I know is it must go with the antique doorknob my wife and I bought in Vermont."

■ A collector of old furniture was bargaining for an old chair.

"It's Queen Anne, sir, I tell you," said the vendor.

"It may be, but how do you know it is?"

"You see these letters, sir—'Q.A.' They stand for 'Queen Anne.'"

"Well," retorted the collector, "if that stands for 'Queen Anne', I've got a door at home that dates back to William the Conqueror!"

- An antique collector passing through a small village stopped to watch an old man chopping wood with an ancient ax. "That's a mighty old ax you have there," he remarked.

  "Yup," said the villager, "it once belonged to George Washington."

  "Not really!" gasped the collector. "It certainly has stood up well."

  "Of course, it's had three new handles and two new heads."

- The overnight millionaire wanted the best of everything. He went into a music shop and asked to see their most expensive violin. The assistant brought out a beautiful instrument, made in 1730.

  "Wait a minute," said the millionaire, "you say this fiddle was made in 1730?"

  "That's right."

  "Then tell me, is the company that made it still in business?"

  "Of course not!" exclaimed the assistant.

  "Then it's no good," decided the millionaire. "What would I do for spare parts?"

Apparel

- The electronic computer saves man a lot of guesswork, but so does a bikini bathing suit.

- Advertisement placed by clothing merchant: *If you buy a suit from us you will soon want one of our topcoats to wear over it.*

- Former Prime Minister David Ben Gurion of Israel disliked formal attire. In his office he wore a pair of slacks and a shirt open at the collar.

  Once, at a diplomatic reception, he had to wear the traditional striped trousers and cutaway. Observing the raised eyebrows, he said apologetically: "Please forgive my appearance. These are my working clothes."

Appreciation

- "Little pictures leave me cold; it's the grand, big canvasses that I like."

  "You're an art critic, I take it?"

  "Not I—I'm a frame maker."

- *Stranger:* "Good morning, doctor, I just dropped in to tell you how much I benefited from your treatment."

  Doctor: "But you're not one of my patients."

  Stranger: "I know. But my uncle was and I'm his heir."

- "How can I ever show my appreciation?" gushed a woman to Clarence Darrow, after he had resolved her legal troubles.

  "My dear woman," replied Darrow, "ever since the Phoenicians invented money there has been only one answer to that question."

Architecture

- In 1875, President Ulysses S. Grant officially opened the bizarre old State Department building with its gingerbread exterior and weird interior decor. A guide, having proudly given Grant a full tour of the building, said, "One thing more, Mr. President. The building is fireproof."

  "What a pity," said the President.

Argument—Arguments

- "You never listen to me," charged one business partner to another.

  "That's because you never say anything worth listening to," the partner responded.

- Convince someone against their will and they remain of the same opinion still.

- There are usually two sides to every argument but no end.

- The quickest way to kindle a fire is to rub two opposing opinions together.

- Individuals who always insist upon having the last word in an argument should remember that sometimes the last word is "ouch!"

Armed Forces

- Why draft married people? They have no fight left in them.

- Have you heard about the captain who blew his top because someone sent him a letter marked *Private*?

- "We get free food, free living quarters, free clothing, free travel, free medical care...why do they have to louse it up with sergeants?"

- Two army privates spotted a dead animal lying alongside a camp road and they stopped to look at it. "The thing has two stripes," said one.

  "That settles it," said the other. "It's either a skunk or a corporal."

- "Just fancy that!" exclaimed a proud mother after reading a letter from her son in the army. "They've promoted our Herbert for being the only one who had the nerve to hit that tough top sergeant. They've made Herbert a court marshall!"

- When a sergeant asked a soldier, who had complained about finding sand in his soup, whether he had joined the army to serve his country or to complain about the food, the soldier replied:

  "I joined the army to serve my country, not to eat it."

- "All you men who like music," the top sergeant called out, "step forward two paces." Six men responded.

  "Now then," the top kick said, "you six get busy and carry that piano to the top floor of the barracks."

- "Well," snarled the tough old sergeant to the private, "I suppose after you get discharged from the Army you'll just be waiting for me to die so you can come spit on my grave."

  "Not me, Sarge," the GI assured him, "once I get out of this army, I ain't never going to stand in line again!"

- An Army recruiting poster in downtown Los Angeles showed three eager-looking soldiers. The first soldier was pictured as saying "I want education." The second: "I want travel." And the third: "I want security." Underneath, some anonymous dog-face had scrawled in big, black block letters: "*I want out!*"

- A rooming house landlord received a phone call from the mother of a college freshman. "Please keep an eye on Albert for me," begged the mother. "See that he gets plenty of sleep and doesn't drink or run around too much."

  "You see," she said in an apprehensive tone, "this is the first time he's been away from home—except for two years in the Marines."

■ A bunch of recruits were having a written examination, and when one of them was asked why he wasn't working, he replied, "Sir, I have neither paper nor pencil."

"Well!" exclaimed the instructor, "What would you think of a soldier who went into battle with neither rifle nor ammunition?"

The recruit thought for a moment, then answered, "I'd think he was an officer, sir."

■ A young man had just finished his tour of duty and had been released from the Air Force and entered the fall semester of a Western university. One morning he was ten minutes late for his nine o'clock class. The professor, knowing the young man was on the GI Bill, bawled him out in front of the class.

"When you were in the service and came in late like this," the professor said, "what did they say to you?"

"When I came in late," the student said, "they just stood up, saluted and said 'How are you this morning, colonel, sir?'"

■ A high-ranking military officer on duty with the Central Intelligence Agency was checking out a brand new electronic computer which the manufacturer had said was capable of answering any question.

Sure enough, no matter how difficult the problem put to it, the electronic machine came up with the answer.

Impressed, the officer wrote out the big question on a piece of paper—"What about World War III?"—and fed it into the computer.

Gears turned, lights blinked, bells rang, and out popped the answer: "Yes."

The officer scratched his head, and then wrote out: "Yes what?"

Again the gears turned, the lights blinked, and bells rang. Out came the tape, and written on it was "Yes, Sir."

■ An old army sergeant was put in charge of a plot of grass in front of administrative headquarters in a camp in Michigan. The sergeant promptly delegated the job to a buck private and told him to water the grass every day at five o'clock. This the private did conscientiously.

One day, however, when there was a terrific thunderstorm, the sergeant walked into the barracks and saw the private doing bunk fatigue.

"What's the matter with you?" the sergeant bellowed. "It's five o'clock and you're supposed to be out watering the grass!"

"But sergeant," the private said, looking confused, "it's raining! Look at that thunderstorm."

"So what!" yelled the sergeant. "You've got a raincoat, haven't you?"

■ An Irish drill sergeant was instructing some recruits in the mysteries of marching movements. He had great difficulty in getting one fellow to halt when the command was given. After explaining and illustrating several times, he approached the recruit, sized him up silently for a couple of minutes, and then demanded his name.

"Casey, sir," was the reply.

"Well, Casey, did ye iver drive a mule?"

"Yis, sir."

"An' what did ye say whin ye wanted him t'stop?"

"Whoa," answered Casey.

The sergeant turned away and immediately put his squad in motion. After they had advanced a dozen paces he bawled out at the top of his voice: "Squad halt! Whoa, Casey!"

Art—Artist—Artists

■ *Friend to artist*: "It's a good portrait, but I don't think it will ever get stolen."

■ The first prize for sculpture in a modern art show went to a curiously shaped piece bearing this sign: "The sculptress made this entirely with her tongue."

Someone questioned the exhibitor, "Who is this talented sculptress?"

"My cow," he answered, "that's her salt block!"

■ The newly-rich woman was going through a "culture" routine and at this particular moment was standing in front of a painting in New York's famous Metropolitan Museum. It was a beautiful oil of a ragged but happy vagabond. "Well!" exclaimed the woman indignantly, "How do you like that? Too broke to buy a decent suit of clothes, but he can afford to go out and get his portrait painted."

- W. Somerset Maugham, a collector of modern paintings, was once asked by a reporter if in his long life he had ever encountered a miracle.

  "The painter Rubens," he replied, "was a miracle."

  The reporter was puzzled. "Do you imply, sir, that Rubens' paintings were miraculous?"

  "Not that," explained Maugham. "But Rubens painted only 2,000 canvasses of which the world now has 3,000 left. That is what I call a miracle."

- Lorado Taft, the great Chicago sculptor, used to tell this story on himself. One blustery, rainy day as he came out of the Art Institute, he saw two nuns across the street. The wind was whipping their robes around them and, as a sculptor, he was fascinated by the line they made. At the time he was working on a piece of sculpture of a mythological figure with robes blown by the wind, so he was delighted to have this example to study. Completely absorbed, he walked along on the opposite side of the street watching them.

  Suddenly he saw that a man was deliberately following the nuns. Profoundly shocked at such an outrageous thing, the moment he could get through the traffic Mr. Taft flew across the street, caught up with the man, grabbed him by the shoulder, whirled him around and said, "How dare you?"

  To his amazement, Taft found himself looking into the face of a fellow sculptor.

  —*Daniel Chester French*

Attire

- If the principal function of dressing is to cover weaknesses, then why don't more people wear hats?

- A beautiful Hollywood actress was trying on a dress in the studio wardrobe department. "I don't like that color," commented the designer. "Now if you'd wear a dress to match those stockings, you'd be a sensation."

  "I certainly would," replied the actress. "I'm not wearing stockings."

- A man came home from work tired, but his eyes lighted up as he stepped inside his house and saw a beautiful layer cake with seven candles on it, on the dining room table. "A birthday cake!" he exclaimed with pleasure. "Whose birthday is it?"

"Oh," replied his wife nonchalantly, "that's for the dress I've got on. It's seven years old today."

■ A staid gentleman was upset by the dress of modern girls at a rodeo.

"Just look at that young person with the short hair and the blue jeans," he remarked to a bystander. "Is it a boy or a girl?"

"It's a girl, she's my daughter!"

"Oh, please forgive me, sir. I had no idea you were her father!"

"I'm not. I'm her mother!"

■ "I want a new suit made," the customer said, "and I want it in a hurry."

The tailor shrugged. "I can make it for you," he said, "but it'll take me thirty days."

"Thirty days! Why, the Lord created heaven and earth in only six!"

"Sure," said the tailor quietly. "And have you taken a look at it lately?"

Attitude

■ There was a man who lived by the side of a busy highway and sold hot dogs for a living.

His hearing had failed him so he rarely listened to the radio, and his eyesight was getting progressively worse so reading the newspaper or magazines became impossible. However, he sold great hot dogs.

His advertising consisted of small signs along the highway telling passers-by how great his hot dogs were. Daily he would stand on the side of the road and verbally advertise, "Hey, stop and buy one of my great hot dogs!" and people bought!

In fact, sales were so good, he soon increased his meat and bun orders. He purchased a larger stove to handle the increased orders and even lengthened his hours to keep up. People even requested his services for family and company picnics. The hot dog business was booming.

Finally, his college-educated son joined the business. Within a few weeks, the son commented, "You know, Dad, the pace of your business is bound to falter. The radio, newspaper, and magazines all indicate we are in the middle of a recession. Times are tough and businesses are faltering all around us."

The father, realizing his son was now an educated business person, was embarrassed that he had been so naive. So he immediately cut back on his meat and bun orders. The advertising signs were torn down and he quit encouraging people passing by to try his delicious hot dogs. In a matter of a few days, his sales drastically fell.

"You're right, son," the father said to his boy. "We certainly are in the middle of tough times. It's a good thing you warned me."

Auction—Auctions—Auctioneering

- I am very lucky at auctions. The last one I went to I made bids on sixteen different things—and didn't get caught once.

- A man finally bought a parrot at an auction after some very spirited bidding.
  "I suppose the bird talks," he said to the auctioneer.
  "Talks?" was the reply. "He's been bidding against you for the past half hour."

Authorship

- If you think no evil, see no evil, and hear no evil, the chances are that you'll never write a best-selling novel.

- Someone once asked Oscar Wilde what he had written that day. "In the morning I put in a comma, in the afternoon I took it out," he replied.

- A struggling author had called on a publisher about a manuscript he had submitted.
  "This is quite well written, but my firm publishes works only by writers with well-known names," said the publisher.
  "Splendid," said the author, "My name's Smith."

- When Garry Moore received a television award for his spontaneity, he turned right around and paid tribute to "the four guys responsible for my spontaneity—my writers." Bishop Fulton Sheen, the next to receive an award said, "I also want to pay tribute to my four writers—Matthew, Mark, Luke and John."

—*Faye Emerson*

■ Announcements of the professor's new book and his wife's new baby appeared almost simultaneously. The professor, when he was congratulated by a friend upon "this proud event in your family," naturally thought of that achievement which had cost him the greater effort, and modestly replied:

"Well, I couldn't have done it without the help of two graduate students."

■ Asked if he had known Mark Twain, the white-bearded proprietor of a roadside stand in Hannibal, Missouri, where the great humorist had spent his boyhood days, replied:

"Sure, I knew him," was the prompt and indignant reply. "And I know just as many stories as he did, too. Only difference is, he writ 'em down."

■ A famous newspaper columnist received a number of manuscripts from a young English writer who asked his advice as to the best channel for marketing his writing.

The columnist sent the manuscript back with this note: "The one channel I can conscientiously recommend as the greatest outlet for articles of this type is the English Channel."

■ The author William Faulkner was asked if there was any possible formula to follow in order to be a good novelist.

His answer: "99% talent, 99% discipline, 99% work. He must never be satisfied with what he does. Always dream and shoot higher than you know you can do. Don't bother to be just better than your contemporaries or predecessors. Try to be better than yourself. An artist is a creature driven by demons."

■ The new dictionary was complete and published, and the lexicographer was being complimented by a group of students. He was becomingly modest about his work.

"I don't know how you can stick at a job like that," said one young man. "It must have been hard, monotonous work."

The great man shrugged. "Nothing to it," he said, "It was just like having a row with my wife—one word led to another."

■ When Stephen Leacock was asked by ambitious would-be authors to impart his magic formula for writing success, he would reply, "It is not hard to write funny stuff. All you have to do is procure a pen and paper, and some ink, and then sit down and write it as it occurs to you."

"Yes, yes," the would-be writer prompted.

"The writing is not hard," Leacock would conclude, "but the occurring—that, my friend, is the difficulty."

- A young woman, interested in writing, met author Joel Sayre at a party.

  "Oh, Mr. Sayre, I wonder if you'd help me out?" she asked. "Tell me, how many words are there in a novel?"

  The author was taken aback but managed a sympathetic smile. "Well, that depends. A short novel would run about 65,000 words."

  "You mean 65,000 words make a novel?"

  "Yes," said Sayre, hesitatingly. "More or less."

  "Well, how do you like that?" shouted the girl gleefully. "My book is finished!"

Automation

- *Exhausted husband to wife*: "Boy, what a day! The electronic brain broke down and we all had to think."

- The purchasing agent faces his toughest decision when he negotiates to buy the machine designed to replace him.

- *Boss to employee*: "It should be a great satisfaction to you, Mr. Simkins, to know that it's costing us $250,000 to replace you with a computer."

B

Baldness

- Man's oldest fallout problem: Baldness.

- Men worry more about losing their hair than their heads.

- The bald-headed man may be ridiculed but he's the first in the group to know when it starts to rain.

- *John*: "Have any of your boyhood hopes been realized?"

Tom: "Yes, one, for sure. When my mother used to comb my hair, I would wish I didn't have any."

- "Where did you get that pretty red hair?" a matron asked a pretty miss at a children's party.

  "I think I got it from Daddy," she replied, "Mommy still has hers."

- For every action there still seems to be an opposite and equal reaction. Those who reach the age when they begin to lose a little on top are at the same time probably gaining a little in the middle.

- "Your hair seems to be getting thin on top, sir," remarked the barber to the man in his chair. "Have you tried our private brand of hair tonic?"

  "No, I haven't," replied the customer, "so it can't be that."

Bank—Banks—Banking

- Bank: an institution where you can borrow money if you can present sufficient evidence that you don't need it.

- "Did you get my check?" inquired Brown of Jones.

  "Yes, twice," replied Jones. "Once from you and once from the bank."

- A businessperson visited his banker and asked: "Are you worried about whether I'll be able to meet my note that comes due next month?"

  "Yes, I must admit that I am somewhat concerned," confessed the banker.

  "Good," said the client. "That's why I'm paying you six percent."

- The burglars had tied and gagged the bank cashier after extracting the combination to the safe and had herded the other employees into a separate room under guard. After they rifled the safe and were about to leave, the cashier made desperate pleading noises through the gag. Moved by curiosity one of the burglars loosened the gag.

  "Please!" whispered the cashier, "Take the books, too—I'm $6,500 short."

- A grizzled old banker, who pioneered in a small Western town, was being interviewed on the subject of his successful career.

"How did you get started in the banking business?" queried the interviewer.

"It was very simple," replied the banker. "I put up a sign reading: BANK. A man came in and gave me $100. Then another came in and handed me $200. By that time my confidence had reached such a point that I decided to put in $50 of my own."

■ A woman in a little New England village called up the First National Bank in her community to arrange for the disposition of a $1,000 railroad bond she owned. The man at the bank to whom she talked asked: "Is this bond for conversion or redemption?"

There was a long pause at the other end of the line. Then the woman asked:

"Am I talking to the First National Bank or the First Parish Church?"

■ Several men in the coffee room were arguing as to who was the greatest inventor. One contended for Stephenson, who invented the railroad; another for Edison; another for Marconi; and still another for the Wright brothers.

Finally one of them turned to a small man who had been listening but who had said nothing.

"What do you think, Mr. Morrison?"

"Well," came the reply with a knowing smile, "whoever invented interest was nobody's fool."

■ A group of California bankers once gave a dinner at which were many prosperous Indians of the section. These Indians had not gone in for bank accounts to any extent, and the object of the dinner was to sound them out. Approaching the richest among them, the host of the dinner remarked, "Chief, you've made lots of money, but never opened an account with us. Why don't you think it over?"

The Chief thought it over right then and there. "When I got money," he said in deep, low tones, "you pay me four percent. When I got no money you charge me eight. I'm tired."

■ "I'll test your sagacity," said the banker to a young man whom he turned down for a loan. "I have one genuine and one artificial eye. If you will point out my genuine eye, I will approve your loan."

The young man gazed into both of the banker's eyes and said: "Your left eye is the good one."

"That's perfect," approved the banker somewhat surprised. "How can you tell?"

"Because I thought I saw a little sympathy in the other one," speculated the young man.

■ A crusty old country banker in the Midwest had, to put it mildly, very little regard for bank examiners. When the Federal Reserve Examiners "dropped in" he made it a point to cooperate as little as possible. If they had to examine the bank, then, by golly, let them do it without any help from him.

The examiners decided to do something about the old curmudgeon. Instead of coming once that year, as was usual, they came a second, a third, and even a fourth time. On their last visit, they noticed a huge sign on the small bank, proclaiming: "This is the best darn bank in the U.S. It's under constant Government supervision."

■ Three bank examiners walked into a leading Chicago bank for their monthly audit. It was nearly nine in the evening when one of them exclaimed, "A shortage of $500,000!"

After a careful checking of the balance sheets the other examiners agreed. Early the following morning the bank was a beehive of investigation. The shortage was soon traced to the Department of Check Cancellations.

The department head rushed up to a new employee who was hanging up her hat, and asked excitedly: "Miss Smith, do you recall cancelling a cash sales check for $500,000 yesterday?"

"Oh, that check," the girl replied, opening her purse. "I took that home last night to show my mother the kind of work I do."

■ One day an Indian came into a bank in Oklahoma and asked about a loan.

"Me want $200."

"And what security have you?"

"Got 200 horses."

This seemed sufficient security and the loan was made.

A short time afterward, the Indian came back with $2,200 in cash, paid off the note and started to leave with the rest of the roll in his pocket.

"Why not let me take care of that money for you?" asked the banker.

Looking the banker straight in the eye, the Indian asked, "How many horses you got?"

■ It was during a financial panic that a farmer went to his bank for some money. He was told that the bank was not paying out money but was issuing cashier's checks instead. He could not understand this and insisted on money.

The officers took him in hand, one after another, with little effect. At last the president tried his hand, and after a long and minute explanation, some inkling of the situation seemed to be dawning on the farmer's mind. Much encouraged, the president said: "You understand, now how it is, don't you, sir?"

"I think I do," admitted the farmer. "It's like this, isn't it? When my baby wakes up at night and wants some milk, I give him a milk ticket."

Bankruptcy

■ In the middle of the depression, the owner of a big shoe factory was summoned by the vice president of the local bank. "About that loan of $200,000," the banker started.

The manufacturer held up a hand. "Mr. James," he asked, "what do you know about the shoe business?"

"Frankly," said the banker, "nothing."

"Better learn it fast," advised the manufacturer, "you're in it."

■ A man called a dozen of his creditors together to tell them that he was about to go into bankruptcy:

"I owe you more than $100,000," he said, "and my assets aren't enough to pay 5 cents on the dollar. So I guess it will be impossible for you to get anything—unless you want to cut me up and divide me among you."

Up spoke one of the creditors: "I move we do it. I'd like to have his gall."

■ A man was making application for employment and asked the personnel manager, "Does your company pay my Blue Cross insurance?"

"No you pay for it; it's deducted from your salary each month," he was informed.

"Last place I worked they paid for it," the applicant said.

"Did they give you a life insurance policy, too?"

"Sure."

"Profit sharing?"

"Sure."

"Two- and three-week vacations?"

"Yes, and they had big bonuses, and gifts for your birthday, and..."

"Why did you leave?"

"The company folded."

Barber—Barbers—Barbershop

- *Barber:* "You say you've been here before? I don't remember your face."

   Customer: "I don't doubt that, It's healed now!"

- "What do you think of the Beatles?" asked the first Beatle fan.

   Replied the second Beatle fan: "I think they're a barbershop quartet that didn't get waited on."

- "Have you got another razor?" asked the man in the chair of his barber.

   "Why?" asked the barber.

   "I'd like to defend myself if I can," answered the customer.

- *Customer:* "Your dog seems fond of watching you cut hair."

   Barber: "Well, it ain't that so much. Sometimes I snip off a bit of a customer's ear."

- A stranger with one arm winced as the barber nicked him again. But the man with the razor chattered on, unnoticing.

   "Haven't you been in here before?" he babbled.

   "No," said the stranger sadly, "I lost this arm in a sawmill."

- A cowhand who was proud of his abundance of curly black hair wore it frontier style. One day his barber teased, "If I cut off those sideburns of yours, I'll bet nobody would recognize you."

   "Could be," mused the cowboy, then added quickly, "and I bet nobody would recognize you, either."

- An Eastern college professor appeared one day in the faculty dining room with his face cut in several places and patched here and there with adhesive tape. In fact, he looked as though he had been shaved with a hoe.

"What's happened to you?" inquired one of the group.

"I was shaved today by a man who took highest honors at Harvard in scholarship," he replied. "He speaks several languages and by many is considered an outstanding authority on French literature."

"Indeed!" said the friend. "But if he is so learned, how come he's a barber?"

"He isn't," said the professor. "I shaved myself today for the first time."

Bargain—Bargains—Bargaining

■ A young matron, shopping, asked a butcher the price of hamburger steak.

"Seventy-nine cents a pound," he replied.

"But at the corner store it is only fifty cents," said the customer.

"Well, why didn't you buy it there?"

"Because they haven't any."

"Oh, I see," said the butcher. "When I don't have it I sell it for forty cents a pound."

■ Late one stormy night, several years ago, a physician was aroused from sleep by a farmer who lived several miles out in the country. The farmer, who had a reputation for being "a little stingy," first inquired how much the doctor charged for country calls.

"Three dollars," snapped the doctor, impatient that the fellow would bargain under such circumstances.

Thereupon the farmer urged the doctor to drive to his home immediately. So the doctor dressed and drove with the farmer to his house with as much speed as the muddy, slippery roads permitted. As soon as they stopped in front of the house, the farmer stepped out of the auto, took three dollars from his pocket and handed them to the doctor.

"But where is my patient?" demanded the physician.

"There ain't none," answered the country man "but that there livery man would have charged me five dollars to bring me out here tonight."

Bible

- A group of executives got into a heated discussion about the Bible. Each one claimed they were more knowledgeable than the other. Finally, one executive challenged another, "I'll bet you don't even know the Lord's Prayer."

  "Oh, that's easy," the other responded. "It's 'now I lay me down to sleep...'"

  "Wow," the first executive said. "You are a lot more knowledgeable than I thought."

Boastfulness

- A group of little girls were boasting of the rank of their respective families. They had passed from clothes to personal appearance, then to interior furnishings, and finally to parental dignity. The minister's little girl boasted:

  "Every package that comes for my papa is marked D.D."

  "And every package that comes for my papa is marked M.D." retorted the daughter of the physician.

  Then followed a look of contempt from the youngest of the party. "Huh," she exclaimed, "every package that comes to our house is marked C.O.D."

- Several hunters were sitting around bragging about the dogs they owned. Noting that an elderly native was listening intently, they laid it on thick.

  "Take my setter," said one man. "When I send him to the store for eggs, he refuses to accept them unless they're fresh. What a nose that dog has!"

  "That's nothing," boasted another. "My springer goes out for cigars and refuses to accept any but my favorite brand. Not only that, he won't smoke any until he gets home and I offer him one."

  "Say, old-timer," said another man turning to the native, "did you ever hear of any dogs as smart as ours?"

  "Just one—my brother's dog," was the reply. "I think he's a bit smarter."

  "How?" he was asked.

  "Well," replied the native, "he runs the store where your dogs trade."

Book—Books

- "I would like a nice book for an invalid," said the little old lady. "Yes, madam," said the clerk. "Something religious?"

  "Er-no," replied the lady, "the doctor told him this morning he was going to get well."

- In a hurry to select a book for a friend's birthday, I was lucky enough to find just what I wanted. As I was about to hand it to the busy clerk, I noticed the book jacket was soiled.

  "Isn't this one a little dirty?" I asked as he took it.

  "Lady," he said impatiently, "I don't know—I haven't had time to read it."

- One day, shortly after Christmas, a friend of Mark Twain paid a visit to the humorist's house. When he entered the library, he noticed a pile of books on the floor.

  "Gifts?" he asked.

  Twain nodded.

  "Why do people always give writers books for gifts?" asked the other. "Don't they think we ever need anything else?"

  "Oh, I like books," said Twain. "Take these heavy books, for example. There's nothing like a heavy book for throwing at noisy cats. And thin books are just the thing to put under shaky tables and chairs. And look at this leather-bound volume. It makes an ideal razorstrop. Books are ideal gifts, I can't get enough of them."

Bore—Bores—Boredom

- Dorothy Parker once visited for a weekend the country estate of some friends. It was so boring to her that she almost immediately sent the following telegram to a friend back home: "Please send me a loaf of bread—and enclose a saw and file."

- The minister, being ill, his wife had been instructed by his attending physician, to take and record periodically his temperature. But through inadvertence or mistake, the minister's wife used a barometer instead of a thermometer. When the doctor called to find out about his patient's condition he asked for a "reading" and received this reply: "Dry and windy."

- An American businessperson, visiting in Mexico, watched an Indian making pottery vases. He asked the price. "Twenty centavos each."

  "And for 100?"

  The native thought it over, then answered: "That will be 40 centavos each."

  The American thought the Indian was making a mistake in his quotation of the price, so he tried again. "And if I bought 1,000 all alike?"

  "All alike? One thousand? Well, then they would cost you 60 centavos apiece."

  "Impossible! Why, you must be insane!"

  "It could be," replied the Indian. "But I'd have to make so many all alike, and I wouldn't enjoy that. So, you see, you would have to pay me well for my work as well as for my boredom."

Borrow—Borrowing

- The quickest way to lose your shirt is to put too much on the cuff.

- *Homemaker (to salesperson at the door):* "I'm not in the market for a vacuum cleaner, but you might try the people next door. We often borrow theirs and it's in terrible condition."

- The entire neighborhood was in its seasonal frenzy of spring gardening. One soiled property owner wearily approached his neighbor and asked, "Hate to bother you, Jones, but could I get back the spade you borrowed from me last weekend?"

  "I'm sorry," Jones replied. "I loaned it to a friend down the block. Do you need it?"

  "Not for myself," said the gardener, "but the fellow I borrowed it from wants it back."

- Every time the man next door headed toward Robinson's house, Robinson knew he was coming to borrow something.

  "He won't get away with it this time," muttered Robinson to his wife. "Watch this."

  "Er, I wondered if you'd be using your power saw this morning," the neighbor began.

  "Gee, I'm awfully sorry," said Robinson with a smug look. "But the fact of the matter is, I'll be using it all day."

"In that case, you won't be using your golf clubs. Mind if I borrow them?"

Bragging

■ An American visitor was rather perturbed because his stories of the wonders of his country made little impression on his English friends. He could not seem to bring home to them the gigantic size of his state or, for that matter, the superior speed of American transport. "You know," he said at last, "you can get into a train in the state of Texas at dawn and twenty-four hours later you'll still be in Texas."

"Ah, yes," politely murmured one of his friends. "We've got some pretty slow trains in this country, too."

Brevity

■ George Bernard Shaw once received an invitation from a celebrity hunter: "Lady X will be at home Thursday between four and six."

The author returned the card; underneath he had written: "Mr. Bernard Shaw likewise."

■ The lesson in newspaper work is constantly "Be brief!" If that order can be filled picturesquely, so much the better and it will not be forgotten.

■ A certain beginner in journalism picked up in a Southern town what seemed to him a "big story". He hurried to the telegraph office and queried the editor of his newspaper: "Column story on _____. Shall I send?"

The answer arrived promptly; "Send 600 words."

This to the enthusiastic correspondent was depressing. "Can't be told in less than 1,200," he wired back.

Then came this reply: "Story of creation of world told in 600. Try it."

Brotherhood—Sisterhood

■ A legend has come out of Germany based on the Nazi persecution of the Jews. A pastor, acting on orders from the Gestapo, said to his congregation: "All of you who had Jewish fathers will leave and not return." A few worshippers rose and left the sanctuary. Again he said: "All of you who had Jewish mothers must go and not return." As before, a few worshippers left. As the pastor looked on, he saw the remaining members of the congregation turn pale. The figure on the cross above the altar had loosed itself and left the sanctuary. Jesus cannot abide in a heart, a home, a church, or a community where prejudices exist.

- A wonderful story is told to illustrate the folly of exclusiveness in worship of a God who made us all and whose tender mercies are over all His works. A black man passed a fashionable church. He thought he would like to worship there, and spoke to the minister about joining the congregation. The minister told him that God did not wish us to change our denominations, that he had better go home and talk this matter over with God. The man returned in a short time. The minister asked him if he had talked it over with God and, if so, what did God say? The man told him: "God said to me, 'Sam, I've been trying to get into that church myself for twenty-five years and ain't had any luck. No use your trying.'"

- It was sleeting overhead and slushy underfoot. People hurried along Forty-second Street with their coat collars up about their ears, hardly glancing at passers-by. A young weary traveller, carrying a heavy valise in one hand and a huge suitcase in the other, hurried toward the Grand Central Station, slipping and skidding as he went.

  Suddenly a strong hand reached out and took the valise while a pleasant voice said: "Let me take one, brother! Bad weather to have to carry things."

  The young man was reluctant, but the stranger insisted, "I'm going your way." All the way to the station they chatted like two old buddies.

  Years later, Booker T. Washington, the famed black educator, said, "That was my introduction to Theodore Roosevelt."

Budget—Budgets

- The workings of the modern budgets are marvelous. Brown and Jones were discussing their respective budgets, when Brown asked: "How do you budget your income, Bill?"

"Well," replied Jones, "it works out this way: 30 per cent for rent, 30 per cent for clothing, 40 per cent for food, medicine and charity, and 20 per cent for amusement and such like."

"But wait a minute, Bill," exclaimed Brown, "that adds up to 120 per cent!"

"Well, that's right," replied Jones. "That's the way the thing works out."

Business

- A new car dealer came upon hard times. He fell so deeply in debt that his banker called him in. After a long, heated visit, the car dealer inquired, "Have you ever been in the car business?"

  "No, I can't say I have," said the banker.

  "Well," said the distressed dealer, "you are now."

- Department store detective: counter spy.

- Don't learn the tricks of the trade—learn the trade.

- New York City businessperson, Norman A. Brodsky, characterizes fast business growth and creative financing with this story:

  A guy goes to the horse track, puts down $2 on the first race, and wins. He bets the pile on the second and wins again. He risks that on the third, and so on. Eventually, he's ahead $800,000 and—what the heck—lets everything ride on the last race. The horse finishes out of the money. When the man gets home, his wife asks how he fared. "I lost $2," he confides.

- Anybody can cut prices, but it takes brains to make a better article.
  —*Philip D. Armour*

- Business is like a wheelbarrow—it stands still unless someone pushes it.

- Sign posted on a closed gasoline service station: WE UNDERSOLD EVERYONE.

- Executive: someone who talks with visitors so the other employees can get their work done.

- During the depression days business was so quiet you would even hear the passing of the dividends.

- A modern employer is one who is looking for people between the ages of 25 and 30 with 40 years' experience.

- *Automobile-manufacturing tycoon to assistant*: "If those traffic jams didn't cause our workers to be late we could make 200 more cars each week."

- Pity the poor businessperson. When the help isn't clamoring for more pay and shorter hours, the customers are yelling for lower prices and better service.

- In the business world, an executive knows something about everything, a technician knows everything about something—and the switchboard operator knows everything!

- The story is told of a community-minded businessperson being honored for his contributions to the community. Grateful citizens gathered for a testimonial dinner to thank the man for his giving spirit. In introducing the well-respected man, the Chamber of Commerce president shared a long list of his accomplishments, including being president of a large manufacturing company, possessing several real estate holdings, having spearheaded a host of economic development projects, and an exhausting list of voluntary investments.

  "Your support is overwhelming," said the honored man when he began to speak. "Many of you are well aware of my accomplishments and that not one of them would have been possible without your help. For I came to this community with the clothes I was wearing and a paper bag containing all my worldly belongings."

  At the close of the speech, a young admirer asked, "What was in the bag?"

  "My million dollar inheritance," came the reply.

- *Department store manager (chiding clerk)*: "What do you mean by arguing with that lady? Remember, the customer is always right!"

  Clerk: "But she said we were swindlers!"

- The cloak and suit manufacturer received a wire from a customer reading: "Cancel our order at once." To which the manufacturer replied: "Regret your order cannot be canceled at once, you will have to await your turn."

- A parking lot owner called all three of his attendants together for a little talk. "Look," he said, "we haven't had one complaint in a week about dented fenders." (He paused to let his words sink in.) "Now you tell me how we can make any money leaving *that* much space."

- *Boss:* "Integrity and wisdom are essential to success in this business. Integrity means when you promise a customer something, keep that promise even if we lose money."
  New employee: "And what is wisdom?"
  Boss: "Don't make such promises."

- A teacher asked those pupils who wanted to go to Heaven to raise their hands. All hands went up except one. The teacher asked the youngster if he didn't want to go to Heaven and he replied that he had heard his father tell his mother that "Business had all gone to Hell" and he wanted to go where the business had gone.

- A company was conducting a survey among its stockholders and asked one of them how she knew that the company was successful and that the management was doing a good job. Her reply was almost a classic. She said, "When I get the annual report, I look at the total assets and the total liabilities. If they are the same, I know that everything is all right."

- A man walked into a dress shop and asked the proprietor how business was.
  "Terrible!" he complained. "I sold only one dress yesterday. And today it's even worse."
  "How could it be worse?" asked his friend.
  "Today she returned the dress she bought yesterday," wailed the proprietor.

- A man was admiring his new suit. His friend asked him what was so wonderful about it. He said, "The wool is from Australia, the buttons from California, the thread from Japan, and the lining from New York." After his friend inquired what was so wonderful about that, the reply was: "Isn't it wonderful that so many people can make a living from a suit that I haven't paid for?"

- Farmer Jones bought Farmer Smith's sorrel mare for $100 cash. Smith got to thinking that since Jones paid the price so willingly, the mare must be worth more. Next day he bought the mare back for $200. Later Jones again bought the mare—for $300. This kept going on until the price went up to $1,500.

Then a horse trader from another county came on the scene and bought the horse from Smith for $2,000. Hearing of this, Jones hurried over to Smith and berated him. "You are a fool, selling that mare. Both of us were making a good living off her!"

■ Seated in a hotel lobby was a party of businesspeople attending a convention. Among them was a man who announced himself as a mind reader.

"I will bet ten dollars with anyone in this group," he said, "that I can tell you what you are thinking about."

"I'll take that bet," said one man.

The mind reader gazed intently into his eyes for a few seconds, and then announced:

"You are thinking of going to the city, buying $10,000 worth of goods, then going home, declaring yourself a bankrupt, and settling with your creditors at ten cents on the dollar."

The merchant did not answer, but reached into his pocket and handed over the ten dollars.

"Ah," said the mind reader, "then I read your mind correctly."

"Not at all," said the man. "But the idea is easily worth the ten dollars."

■ Three timid boys entered the village hardware store. The gruff proprietor said to the oldest, "What do you want, Zeke?"

"A dime's worth of BB shot, please."

The old man climbed a ladder, brought down the shelf box that contained the air-rifle shot, made up the packet and returned the box to the shelf above. Then he asked the second boy, "What do you want, Tim?"

"A dime's worth of BB's, please," was the meek answer.

"Why didn't you say so before?" said the old man irritably, as he went for the ladder again. He made up the packet as before, and then turned to the third.

"And do you want a dime's worth of BB's too?" he demanded.

"No," replied Joe hesitatingly.

The old man climbed laboriously to the shelf again and deposited the box of shot. Then he returned to the counter.

"Well, my boy, what do you want?" he demanded of Joe.

"A nickel's worth of BB shot," said Joe.

■ A horse dealer bought a horse which attracted the attention of a farmer. "Want to sell?" the farmer asked.

"Well, I bought this horse for my own use, but there's no reason I shouldn't sell him if we can agree on a price."

"How much do you want for him?"

"I paid $150 for him and I think I'm entitled to a profit of $50. If you want him for $200, he's yours."

The deal was made and the horse was delivered. The animal was just as represented and proved satisfactory to the new owner, Imagine the latter's surprise, however, when he received a check of $50 from the dealer, with a note which said: "I told you I paid $150 for that horse. On consulting my records I find I was mistaken. I paid only $100 for him. I told you my profit was $50, therefore I'm sending you $50 to make the deal right."

Although this dealer was merely doing business in harmony with his principles, and expected no special reward for having sent that $50 check, the farmer who got the check was so pleased that he told the story over and over and it proved to be the best advertisement the dealer received. He could not have bought better advertising for a hundred $50 notes used in any other way.

C

Coffee Break—Coffee Breaks

■ The trouble today with staying home from work is that you have to drink coffee on your own time.

■ A young steno rushed into the office fifteen minutes late on the first morning she reported for work on a new job.

"Young lady," the supervisor said, "you're late!"

"Oh no, sir," she replied, "I just took my coffee break before I came in."

■ An office worker, loafing at the breakfast table, looked up languidly from the morning paper and asked his wife for another cup of coffee.

"Another cup of coffee!" she exclaimed in surprise. "Aren't you going to the office today?"

"Good lord!" the man exclaimed. "I thought I was at the office!"

Collaboration

- One speaker at a recent meeting of the American Chemical Society was asked how he and a collaborator had worked. "It was a 50—50 proposition," the man replied. "I thought up the problem and he solved it."

Commitment

- As president of the Black Leadership Council, the Reverend Robert Ard explained the difference between involvement and commitment this way: "When you look at a plate of ham and eggs, you know the chicken was involved, but the pig was committed."

Communication

- As Secretary of Commerce, Malcolm Baldridge enjoyed telling how a high ranking official responded to an employee's request for a raise by saying: "Because of the influctuational predisposition of your position's productive capacity as juxtaposed to government standards, it would be monetarily injudicious to advocate an increment."

  Confused, the employee said, "I don't get it."

  The supervisor responded, "That's right."

Competition

- He had won many races and was boasting of his speed and achievements when a man sitting near him interrupted.

  "I'll race you any day," said the stranger, "and you'll never pass me if you give me a couple of yards start and let me choose the course."

  The athlete looked at his challenger, a short and rather stout man, and laughed.

  "I'll bet you twenty to one I'll win," he returned. "Where's the course?"

  "Up a ladder," answered the fat man.

  —S.C. Mitchell

- Several years ago on a bright, sunny afternoon a New York street hawker was crying his wares. His cart was filled with writing paper and envelopes. In a loud voice he yelled:

  "Here y'are! Box o' paper an' twenty-five envelopes—on'y one dime!"

  Suddenly his yells were drowned out by even louder ones, and another hawker, crowding the first one out of the way, jostling him rudely, shouted as he pushed along a bigger cart, also filled with stationery:

  "Five cents—on'y a nickel—box o' paper an' twenty-five envelopes! On'y one nickel!"

  The carts came near colliding. The two men glared at each other. The spirit of competition ran high, and the people, drawn by the shouts, gathered around the two hawkers.

  Finding that the two kinds of paper were identical, the people bought the cheaper sort. The nickel man did a terrific business, while the dime man shouted on lustily, to no avail.

  Finally the sales ceased. Everybody had bought enough paper to last a year. The dime man departed first, and the nickel man left a few minutes later. I followed them to see a repetition of the rival sales in the next street.

  There, to my amazement, the dime man was waiting around the corner, and as he piled a lot of his stock on the other's nearly empty cart, I heard him say with a chuckle, "It works fine, Bill, don't it?"

- Competition can be compared to the two hikers who spotted a mountain lion stalking them. One of the hikers calmly sat down, took off his hiking boots and began putting on his running shoes. "What good are those shoes going to do you?" asked his buddy. "You can't outrun a mountain lion!" Lacing up his tennies, the friend responds, "I don't have to outrun the lion. I figure staying ahead of you will do just fine."

Compromise

- A small community in the midwest was considering the development of a municipal utility. Citizens were split in their attitude towards this controversial issue. Proponents from each side were doing their best to persuade middle-of the-roader citizens to their way of thinking. One homeowner found a way to refrain from making a commitment.

"Are you in favor of the city council's proposal to develop a municipal utility?" asked his neighbor.

"Well, some of my friends think it's a good idea," responded the man. "Other friends are opposed to the plan. Me? I'm for my friends."

■ "I would be happy to compromise," cried the irate wife, "if I were ever wrong. But how can I compromise when I am always right?"

■ "I had a terrible argument with the electric company over our bills," she told her husband when he got home from work.

"Who won?" he asked.

"We compromised. They don't get any more money, we don't get any more electricity."

■ "Darling," scolded the mother, "you shouldn't always keep everything for yourself. I have told you before that you should let your brother play with your toys half of the time."

"I've been doing it," Darling replied. "I take the sled going downhill and he takes it going up."

Construction

■ A contractor promised to complete repairs within forty-eight hours. However, the homeowner waited four days before the crew even showed up. "You are now two days past your promise," commented the irate homeowner.

"What do you mean?" asked the contractor. "I told you forty-eight hours. That's six days," he snapped. "We work eight-hour days."

Cosmetics

■ *One teen-age girl to another*: "I developed an entirely new personality yesterday—but my father made me wash it off."

■ The matron walked to the department store information booth and asked the pretty young woman to direct her to the perfume counter.

"Just walk this way," she said, taking the lead.

"Humpf!" the matron said. "If I could walk that way I wouldn't need perfume."

Creditor—Creditors

■ "There's a man outside," said the secretary to her boss, "who wants to see you about a bill you owe him. He wouldn't give his name."
"What does he look like?"
"Well, he looks like you had better pay him."

Customer Service

■ Those who enter to buy, support me. Those who come to flatter, please me. Those who complain, teach me how I may please others so that more will come. Only those hurt me who are displeased but do not complain. They refuse me permission to correct my errors and thus improve my service.

—Marshall Field

■ Several years ago, a Blondie cartoon pictured Dagwood complaining to the cook that the chicken croquettes he had been served were too small. After tasting one he added, "and they taste horrible." The quick thinking server responded, "Then you're lucky they are small."

■ Technical assistance research programs determined that it costs five times more to go out and get a new customer than it does to maintain a customer you already have. Additional research indicated that fixing customers' problems fast and completely is a key to retaining customers. Here's why:

91 percent of those who complain won't come back.

Each dissatisfied customer will tell an average of 9–10 others.

If the problem is fixed within forty-eight hours, 82–95 percent of these customers will return. In fact, a well-handled problem generally breeds more loyalty than before the problem occurred.

■ A weary traveling salesperson entered the beautiful hotel lobby and requested lodging for the night.
The hotel clerk responded, "I'm sorry but all of our rooms are occupied for tonight."
The traveler probed, "You mean to tell me if the President of the United States walked in, you would not have room for him?"

"Well, of course we would find room for the President," said the clerk.

"He is traveling overseas," quipped the traveler, "so why don't you let me have his room?"

- Returning change to a customer, the sales clerk mumbled something. "I'm sorry," said the customer, "I didn't hear what you said."

"I said have a great day," snapped the clerk. "What are you, deaf or something?"

- We believe in serving the customer properly and doing the job right...if in doing that, we wind up being number one in more places, so be it.

—*Donald L. Korn, Avis, Inc.*

- After-Christmas complaints and returns flooded the department store. One customer service person patiently listened to a disgruntled customer complaining non-stop about an item she had purchased. Unable to get a word in edgewise, the service representative finally interrupted with: "I'm sorry for the inconvenience we have caused you. If I were to refund your money, give you a free replacement, and then commit suicide, would that be helpful?"

- The story is told of a flower shop in a large mall crowded with customers waiting for attention. The phone rang at the check-out counter and the caller ordered a dozen long-stem roses. The sales clerk asked where the flowers should be delivered.

"Don't bother sending them," said the customer. "Just bring them to the counter. I'm calling from a pay phone just outside your store."

- The quality of any product or service is what the customer says it is.

—*James Balkcom*

- Sol Polk is often referred to as the appliance king of Chicago. The reason is quite simple. Sol began with nothing and two decades later sells $60 million worth of appliances a year. Quality customer service is given credit for his tremendous success. "Customers," says Sol, "should be treated like they are guests in my home."

- A business exists to create a customer.

  —Peter Drucker

- Customer needs have an unsettling way of not staying satisfied for very long.

  —Karl Albrecht/Ron Zemke

- John Barrier didn't react kindly to unkind customer service. He walked into a bank in Spokane Washington to cash a $100 check and then asked a receptionist to validate his 60-cent parking slip. Unimpressed with her customer's dirty construction clothes, she refused, saying he hadn't conducted a transaction. "You must make a deposit," she said, "before I can validate your ticket."

  "I am considered a substantial depositor," Mr. Barrier responded.

  The receptionist provided a blank stare.

  "May I see the manager?" asked Barrier. The manager also refused his request.

  Needless to say, this was becoming a frustrating experience and he had had enough. John Barrier threatened to pull his deposits of $2 million plus unless he received an apology. It never came.

  The result? Listen to John Barrier, "...the next day I went over and the first amount I took out was $1 million. But if you have $100 in a bank or $1 million," he says, "I think they owe you the courtesy of stamping your 60-cent parking ticket."

- *Landlord*: "You didn't pay the rent for last month."

  Tenant: "No? Well, I suppose you'll hold me to your agreement?"

  "Agreement! What agreement?"

  "Why, when I rented you said I must pay in advance or not at all."

- Artist James McNeil Whistler often lived beyond his means. As a result, he was hounded by creditors. Their presence caused him no distress. Rather, he treated them with the utmost cordiality.

  Once, when a persistent creditor called at the artist's home to collect a bill, he was served champagne.

  "If you cannot afford to pay your bills," he demanded with some asperity, "how can you afford to drink champagne?"

"Your anger is too hasty, sir" replied Whistler. "I assure you I haven't paid for this either."

D

Dance—Dancing

- Two dogs were watching a twist dance. After a while one looked at the other and said, "When I act like that they give me worm pills."

- A young girl took her grandfather to a disco party, and while they were watching the dancers she said, "I'll bet you never saw dancing like that when you were young."
  "Once," replied the grandfather, "and the place was raided."

- A social director at a large Honolulu hotel has devised a simple set of instructions for mainland tourists who want to learn the hula. "It's very easy," he explains. "You simply put some grass on one hip, some more grass on the other hip. Then you rotate the crops."

- Two tramps asked a farmer for a meal, and were told that they would indeed have one —if they would fill the woodshed with freshly-chopped kindling. Reluctantly, the tramps agreed.
  After an hour or so, the farmer wandered out to the woodshed to see how the boys were doing with their labors. Rounding a corner of the shed, he was greeted by the amazing sight of one of the tramps executing a series of ballet-type steps and gymnastics. The farmer was stunned.
  "Cricky!" he exclaimed to the other tramp, who was leaning on the ax handle and taking great interest in his companion's gyrations. "I didn't know your friend was an acrobat."
  "Neither did I," replied the second tramp, "until I cracked him on the shin with this here ax."

Debt—Debts

- If one wants to get out and stay out of debt he should learn to act his wage.

Debtor—Debtors, *See also* Creditor—Creditors

- Running into debt isn't so bad. It's running into creditors that hurts.

- Be careful about lending a friend money. It may damage her memory.

- "Well, thank goodness they're giving up on this bill—this says it's their final notice."

- The young couple going over their monthly bills finally were down to the last two.

  "Gosh, honey," said the husband, "we're practically broke. I don't know which to pay—the electric company or the doctor."

  "Oh, the electric company, of course," answered the wife. "After all, the doctor can't shut off your blood."

- Honoré de Balzac, French novelist who was always in debt, once received a short prison sentence for trying to avoid military service.

  One morning he was visited by a friend, who was surprised to find the writer in a jovial mood.

  "Why are you so cheerful?" asked the friend. "Do you find prison so pleasant?"

  "Most pleasant," replied Balzac, "My creditors can't bother me here."

- A man in the garment business sent a mild dunning letter to a young woman who had fallen behind in her payments on a fur coat. In part, the letter read: "What would your neighbors think, if we found it necessary to come and take back your fur coat?"

  Several days later the collection manager received this reply: "I have taken the matter up with my neighbors as you suggested, and they think it would be a lousy trick."

Decision-Making

- Lee Iacocca's ability to make tough decisions and make them work has become a personal trademark. Speaking on management, Iacocca once said: "If I had to sum up in one word what makes a good manager, I'd say decisiveness. You can use the fanciest computers to gather the numbers, but in the end you have to set a timetable and act. And I don't mean rashly. I'm sometimes described as a flamboyant leader and a hip-shooter, a fly-by-the-seat-of-the-pants operator. But if that were true, I could never have been successful in this business."

Dentist—Dentists—Dentistry

- "How is your sore tooth coming along?"
  "Oh, it's driving me to extraction!"

- "I was so cold last night I couldn't sleep. I just lay there and shivered."
  "Did your teeth chatter?"
  "I don't know—we don't sleep together."

Doctor—Patient

- *Executive to his physician*: "I just can't pay your bill, Doc—I slowed down just as you told me to, and I lost my job!"

- *Doctor*: "That check you gave me on your last visit came back."
  Patient: "Sorry, Doc, but so did my arthritis."

- *Doctor*: "Madam, I'd like to give you a thorough examination. Please take off your clothes."
  Patient: "But Dr. Smith found me perfect this morning."
  Doctor: "Yes, he told me."

- The first aid specialist, instructing a class of Girl Scouts, asked: "Why does a surgeon wear a mask while performing an operation?"
  One little girl replied: "So if he makes a mess of it, the patient won't know who did it."

- "Your heart is quite sound. With such a heart you ought to live to be seventy."
  "But, doctor, I am seventy."
  "There! What did I tell you?"

- Every chair in the doctor's waiting room was filled and some patients were standing. There was desultory conversation, but after a while silence fell and the group waited—waited—waited. Finally an old man stood up wearily and remarked: "Well, guess I'll go home and die a natural death."

■ The doctor's new secretary, a conscientious woman, was puzzled by an entry in the doctor's notes on an emergency case: "Shot in the lumbar region," it read. After a moment she brightened and, in the interest of clarity, typed into the record: "Shot in the woods."

■ A man went to see a doctor complaining that he could think of nothing but girls.

"You have to stop that," the doctor said, "or you'll lose your hearing."

"Is that so?" asked the patient.

"What did you say?" asked the doctor.

■ "Doc," he said, "if there's anything wrong with me, don't give me a long scientific name. Say it so I can understand it."

"Very well," the doctor agreed, "you're lazy."

"Thanks, doc, now give me the scientific name so I can tell my boss."

■ A doctor examining an attractive new patient, beamed, "Mrs. Atherton, I've got good news for you."

The patient said, "Pardon me, it's Miss Atherton."

"Oh," said the doctor. "Well, Miss Atherton, I've got bad news for you."

■ *Mike*: "What made you join the police force?"

Pat: "My doctor told me I should get more exercise."

Mike: "What has getting more exercise got to do with being a police officer?"

Pat: "Why should I walk on my own time when I can be a police officer and get paid for it?"

■ "But, doctor," said the worried patient, "are you sure I'll pull through? I've heard of cases where the doctor has made a wrong diagnosis, and treated someone for pneumonia who has afterward died of typhoid fever."

"Nonsense," spluttered the affronted physician. "When I treat a patient for pneumonia, he dies of pneumonia."

■ During one of last winter's worst snow storms the doctor's phone rang late at night. A man wanted him to make a house call on his wife. The doctor said he would dress at once and explained that his own car was in the garage for repairs. He asked the man to drive over and pick him up.

"What!" shouted the caller. "In this weather!"

■ A physician had just finished checking a patient who was well past middle age. "Well, old man," he said with a smile. "I can't find a thing wrong with you, but I do recommend that you give up about half of your love life."

After a long pause, the patient replied, "Which half should I give up, doc, thinking about it or talking about it?"

■ A doctor told the patient she had a fibroid tumor and that he would have to operate immediately. "Don't worry," he said, "everything will be all right."

"But how can you be so positive," she inquired, "when it is known that 14% die under that operation?"

"My dear lady," explained the surgeon, "my 14% have already died."

■ A doctor called on a patient several times, but the patient was unhappy. On the last visit he announced that he had called in another doctor.

"And what's more," said the patient, "he told me your diagnosis is all wrong."

"Is that so?" snapped the doctor. "Well, the autopsy will show who is right."

■ "Are you medical or surgical?" asked one small boy of another in the hospital ward.

"I don't know," replied the youngster.

The questioner was scornful, having been a patient in the hospital for some months. Condescendingly, he undertook to make his meaning plainer for the sake of the lower intelligence of his less quick-witted companion: "Were you sick when you came in, or did they make you sick after you got here?" he inquired.

■ "Have you been to any other doctor before you came to me?" asked the grouchy doctor.

"No, sir," replied the patient, meekly. "I just went to a druggist."

"You went to a druggist?" exclaimed the doctor. "That shows how much sense some people have! And what idiotic advice did the druggist give you?"

"He told me to come and see you," replied the patient.

■ A local doctor became quite popular overnight when he was "written up" in a large city paper which told of his many years of service, achievements, etc. As he was approached one morning soon afterward by a middle-aged woman, she beamed at him and, wanting to impress him as being an acquaintance, she gushed:

"Oh, doctor. I guess you don't remember me. Twenty years ago you came to see me at home and told me to stay in bed until you called back again. But you never came back!"

The doctor, being equal to the occasion, answered rather briskly. "Did I? Well then, what are you doing out of bed?"

■ "Medicine won't help you any," the doctor told the elderly patient. "What you need is a complete rest and a change of living. Get away to some quiet country place for a month. Go to bed early, eat more roast beef, drink plenty of good rich milk, and smoke just one cigar a day."

A month later the patient walked into the doctor's office. He looked like a new man and the doctor told him so.

"Yes, doctor, your advice certainly did the business. I went to bed early and did all the other things you told me. But say, doctor, that one cigar a day almost killed me at first. It's no joke starting to smoke at my age."

■ A certain doctor in the Middle West has received many compliments about his work from patients he has helped. Yet he likes most to remember one bit of tribute that was paid to his deceased father, who had also been a doctor.

Shortly after his father's funeral, the young doctor had stopped to visit a patient, a little boy about four. As the physician was about to leave, the little fellow called him back.

"Doctor, is God very sick?" the child asked anxiously.

The doctor's brow wrinkled in bewilderment. "Why, God never gets sick," he said a trifle brusquely. "How did you happen to ask me that?"

"'Cause your father died, and I guess God must have sent for him," the little boy replied.

■ The doleful-looking customer ambled up to the bar. "Six double whiskeys, please," he said.

The bartender said: "Yes, sir," and poured a measure of liquor into each of six glasses.

"And line them up in front of me, will you?" asked the customer.

Doing as he was bid, the bartender said: "That will be sixteen dollars and fifty cents, sir."

The customer handed him seventeen dollars and said "Keep the change."

He tossed down his throat the contents of the first glass in the line. He repeated the process with the third and fifth glasses. Then saying "Good day," he turned to walk away.

"Excuse me," said the bartender, "but you have left three glasses untouched."

"Yes, I know," said the customer. "The doctor said he didn't mind my taking an odd drink."

- A man sought medical aid because he had popped eyes and a ringing in the ears. A doctor looked him over and suggested removal of his tonsils. The operation resulted in no improvement, so the patient consulted another doctor who suggested removal of the man's teeth. The teeth were extracted still the man's eyes popped and the ringing in his ears continued.

A third doctor told him bluntly, "You've got six months to live." In that event, the doomed man decided he'd treat himself right while he could. He bought a flashy car, hired a liveried chauffeur, had the best tailor in town make him thirty suits, and decided even his shirts would be made to order.

"Okay," said the shirtmaker, "let's get your measurement. Hmm, 34 sleeve, 16 collar—"

"Fifteen," the man said.

"Sixteen collar," the shirtmaker repeated, measuring again.

"But I've always worn a 15 collar," said the man.

"Listen," the shirtmaker said, "I'm warning you. You keep on wearing a 15 collar and your eyes will pop and you'll have a ringing in your ears."

Do-It-Yourself

- The trouble with life is that you're halfway through it before you realize it's one of those do-it-yourself deals.

- A fellow who had been doctoring himself out of a medical book for many years finally succumbed. The cause of death: a typographical error.

- Parents nowadays are too busy even to punish their kids! Mothers are running to bridge parties. Fathers are running off to golf courses and bowling alleys. Before they leave the house, they just say: "Son, we left a strap on the bed. If you do something wrong, hit yourself six times."

Double Meaning

- Dr. Emil G. Hirsch, one of the outstanding rabbis of his day and known for his sharp tongue and wit, once rather terrified an early teen-ager whose mother and father he had united in marriage, by saying to her: "I married your mother but I am not your father."

Dreams

- Tom Monaghan is a dreamer. From as far back as his early teen years, he cherished a dream that he would someday own the Detroit Tigers. Being an orphan from a poor family in Michigan presented a significant roadblock but couldn't strip him of his burning desire.

  Monaghan attended college for a short time but then dropped out to start a small pizza establishment in 1960. With a dreamer leading the way, Monaghan's Domino's Pizza grew to become the world's largest pizza delivery company. With annual sales now exceeding $2 billion in 4,100 outlets, Monaghan has spearheaded a successful course to achieving his dreams. And yes, he did purchase the Detroit Tigers baseball team in 1983 for $53 million.

  Tom Monaghan summarizes his success with a simple, yet dynamic belief that, "dreaming is the greatest preparation for wealth."

Druggist—Druggists—Drug Store

- A young bride walked into a drug store and approached the clerk timidly.

  "The baby tonic you advertise—" she began, "does it really make babies bigger and stronger?"

"We sell lots of it," replied the druggist, "and we've never had a complaint."

"Well, I'll take a bottle," said the bride after a moment, and went out. In five minutes she was back. She got the druggist into a corner and whispered into his ear:

"I forgot to ask about this baby tonic, who takes it—me or my husband?"

- "Who is the best lawyer in town?"
  "Ferris Brown when he is sober."
  "And who is the second best lawyer in town?"
  "Ferris Brown when he is drunk."

E

Economics

- The 1980 Presidential Campaign contained a heavy emphasis on economic issues. Ronald Reagan warned of the coming of another depression if America continued in its present path. President Carter reacted, "That shows how much he knows. This is a recession." That reaction gave Reagan, the communicator, a platform comment to build his campaign on. Reagan responded, "If Mr. Carter wants a definition, I'll give him one. Recession is when your neighbor loses his job, depression is when you lose yours, and recovery will be when Jimmy Carter loses his."

Employer—Employee—Employment

- If coffee breaks get much longer, employees will be late for quitting time.

- Millions are idle, but it's comforting to know that most of them have jobs.

- Always laugh heartily at the jokes your boss tells—it may be a loyalty test.

- The nearest to perfection most people ever come is when filling out an employment application.

- A secretary soon to become a mother sent her resignation: "Dear Boss: I'm getting too big for this job."

- Among the worries of today's business executives is the large number of unemployed still on the payroll.

- He told her he was a diamond cutter. Boy, was she impressed until she found out he mowed the grass at Yankee Stadium.

- When you've just plain goofed and the boss wants to know why, there are a lot worse answers than a straightforward "No excuse, sir."

- When a guy goes around saying he doesn't care about money, there is always some so-and-so who's willing to believe him. Like the boss.

- *Company president to personnel manager*: "Search the organization for an alert, aggressive young person who could step into my shoes— and when you find him/her *fire* them."

- *Boss (to chronically late office assistant)*: "Instead of giving you a gold watch when you retire in forty-five years, we have decided to give you an alarm clock right now."

- *Boss*: "Why are you carrying only one board when other men are carrying two?"
  Laborer: "Maybe they're too lazy to make a second trip."

- A Chicago woman who found her housekeeper unsatisfactory advertised in a newspaper for a new one, under a box number, and received only one reply. From her housekeeper.

- "Sir," said the timid employee, "my wife said I was to ask you for a raise."
  "Good," said the boss, "I'll ask my wife if I can give you one."

- The recently graduated college man, a thoroughly modern youth, was asked if he was looking for work.
  The young man pondered the question briefly, and then replied: "Not necessarily, but I would like a job."

- The president of the firm was travelling to a nearby city on an early morning train. Going into the dining car he found a seat, summoned the steward, and said, "I'd like to try that $6 breakfast my employees always report on their expense accounts after they've ridden on this train."

■ At the end of her first day on the job, a new secretary inquired of her bookkeeper, "Doesn't that sourpuss boss of ours ever laugh aloud?"

"Only," sighed the bookkeeper, "when we ask him for a raise."

■ The room was small, dim, and misty with pungent incense as the wrinkled Gypsy woman looked up from her crystal ball at the man seated before her. "I will answer any two questions for $50."

"Isn't that price rather high?" asked the man.

"Yes, it is," came the reply. "Now what's the second question?"

■ A rich man was hiring a chauffeur for his car. He asked each applicant how close he could drive to a certain cliff without toppling over. "One foot," said one. "Six inches," said another. "Three inches," answered another. But another declared: "Faith, and I'd keep as far away from the place as I could."

"Consider yourself hired," was the reply.

■ A Western rancher had asked the district superintendent to have a pastor assigned to his community.

"How big a man do you want?" asked the superintendent.

"Well, Elder," the wiry, tanned man replied, "we're not overly particular, but when he's on his knees we'd like to have him reach heaven."

■ James Byrnes visited a friend in a small South Carolina town. The friend explained he wanted his ten-year-old son to meet Mr. Byrnes and had sought to induce the little leaguer to remain by explaining that their guest served as representative, senator, assistant to the president, Secretary of State, Justice of the Supreme Court, and governor of South Carolina.

But the youngster headed for his baseball game after exclaiming, "Daddy, from what you say there's something wrong with the fellow. He couldn't hold a job."

■ A nervous gentleman who had been required to forfeit his driver's license some years previously, always blamed his troubles on the unpredictability of women drivers. Naturally his wife's handling of the family car gave him fits. He decided to end this source of family argument by hiring an expert chauffeur.

"I want a man who doesn't trust women drivers," he explained to an applicant. "In fact, I want a man so careful that he won't trust anyone."

"I'm just your man," the applicant replied promptly. "I'm so doggone careful I even want my salary in advance."

- Two judges of Cook County died and took different routes to their destinations. When one judge got to Heaven, he immediately called the other judge and said, "How do you like it down there?"

"Fine," said the second judge. "All we have to do is ascend the bench at 11:00 a.m. Everybody down here gets an immediate trial. We don't work more than fifteen minutes a day. By the way, how is everything upstairs?"

"Terrible," said the first judge. "We get on the bench at 8:00 a.m. and don't get through with our Court Call until 10:00 or 11:00 at night. If you think the Cook County Calendar is bad, you should see our Calendar. The plaintiff can't get a trial for about ten to twenty years."

"How come you have to work so hard?" asked the second judge.

"Well, to tell you the truth," replied the first judge, "we have a terrific shortage of judges up here."

Example

- Des Moines, Iowa city council person, Michael McPherson, was notified that motorists were speeding through a local intersection and that several serious accidents had already occurred. Using his political influence, McPherson convinced the local police department to set up a radar unit there. One of the motorists caught in the radar trap was McPherson, who was ticketed for going 45 m.p.h. in a 35 m.p.h. zone.

Experience

- If we could sell our experiences for what they cost us, we'd all be millionaires.

  —*Abigail Van Buren*

Expert—Experts

- Be careful about calling yourself an expert. One definition holds that an "ex" is a has-been, and a "spurt" is a drip under pressure.

- *First woman*: "What does your husband work at?"
  Second woman: "He's an efficiency expert on a big railroad."
  First woman: "Efficiency expert? What are his duties?"
  Second woman: "It's hard to say, exactly, but if I did it, they'd call it nagging."

F

Facts

- Architect Norman Foster completed the design and construction of a new building in the English countryside. Foster invited the renowned philosopher, inventor, and architect Buckminster Fuller, to tour the new development. Prior to Fuller's visit, Foster told his staff to anticipate every question Buckminster Fuller (his friends called him Bucky) might ask. As the two professionals approached the massive structure, Norman reviewed every component, angle and architectural detail.

  Bucky quietly enjoyed the tour of this impressive structure. As they exited the front door, he turned to Norman and asked simply, "How much does it weigh?"

Farm—Farmer—Farming

- A novice young farmer was looking for some advice and asked an experienced farmer, "What would be good to plant in an area that gets very little rain, has too much late afternoon sun, has clay soil, and lies on a rocky ledge?" Replied the farmer, "How about a flag pole?"

- A farmer was explaining to a city dweller how it happened that all the costs of food had gone up.

  "When a farmer has to know the botanical name of what he grows, the entomological name of the insects which try to destroy it, and the pharmaceutical name of the stuff used to spray it, somebody's got to pay for it."

- A hardware merchant became curious when, week after week, a certain farmer came in and bought several hammers. Finally he asked why.

    "Oh," said the farmer, "I sell them to folks in my neighborhood for $1 apiece."

    "But, man," protested the dealer, "that doesn't make sense. You're paying me $10 each for the hammers."

    "I know, I know," conceded the farmer, "but it beats farming."

Furniture

- A bubbly young woman walked into the furniture store and sought out one of its decorators. She wanted advice on how to augment her present furnishings. "What," asked the decorator, "is the motif—Modern, Oriental, Provincial, Early American?"

    "Well," was the frank reply, "we were married only recently, so the style of our furniture is sort of Early Matrimony—some of his mother's and some of my mother's."

Giving

- At fifty-three years old, he was wealthy and successful but also a wreck of a man. Those who knew him best said he lacked a sense of humor, perspective, and the joy of living. Throughout his illustrious business career, John D. Rockefeller said, "I never placed my head upon the pillow at night without reminding myself that my success might only be temporary." Here he was, the richest man in the world, and yet the most miserable as well. Physical, mental, and emotional distress haunted him, but then a change took place. Rockefeller's definition of success changed. He became a giver rather than an accumulator. He began giving millions of dollars away through the newly formed Rockefeller Foundation. Rockefeller lived the last forty-five years of his life with a revitalized spirit, dedicated to fighting disease and ignorance around the world.

- The businessperson had just handed his youthful visitor a dollar, for which he received an "associate membership" card in the local boy's club.

"Now that I'm a member," the businessperson said, "just what are my rights and privileges?"

After thinking the matter over carefully, the boy replied, "Well, it gives you the right to contribute again next year."

Goals—Goal-Setting

- An executive was being probed concerning his corporation's success.

    "Sir, does the company set goals?"

    "Yes, on an annual basis," the executive replied. "We set goals for the coming year as well as more futuristic goals."

    "How far into the future are your long-range goals?" asked one curious interviewer.

    "One hundred years," responded the executive.

    "What would you say is the key for achieving them?"

    "Patience," he replied, "and a lot of it."

- Babe Ruth was hired to hit home runs, and needless to say, he did. The most memorable of his 714 home runs was when he "called his shot." The bases were loaded, and there were two strikes against him. It was a crucial inning. Suddenly, Babe stepped out of the batter's box, raised his bat, and pointed it to the centerfield stands, indicating to the crowd that the ball was coming their way. The pitch came across the plate. He swung. The rest is history. The ball flew exactly where he had pointed.

    Reporters approached Babe Ruth after the game. "That was a pretty lucky homer," they indicated. "Not at all," replied Babe Ruth, "I intended for that hit to go right there."

H _____

Hotel—Hotels

- A pro football player was fined $100 by his coach for breaking training. He had gone to a party the night before the big game.

    "Don't think I don't know about that hotel episode in Detroit," the manager roared.

"You're way off!" retorted the husky halfback. "There ain't no Hotel Episode in Detroit."

■ A man found bedbugs in his bed, and as he checked out of the hotel complained about them to the manager. Several days later he received a cordial letter explaining that no matter how careful they were, things like this happened every once in a while. They thanked him for calling it to their attention and hoped he would accept their apology. And he would have done so, except that somebody had forgotten to detach a little slip that said, "Send this character the bedbug letter."

Husband—Wife

■ An insurance company, upon receiving a claim from a woman, asked her for some additional evidence concerning the husband's death.

After a good deal of correspondence, the firm received the following letter from the widow:

"I am having such a lot of trouble getting my money that sometimes I actually wish my husband were not dead."

I

Identification—Identity

■ Artist Pablo Picasso surprised a burglar at work in his new chateau. The intruder got away, but Picasso told the police he could do a rough sketch of what the thief looked like. On the basis of the drawing, the police arrested a mother superior, the minister of finance, a washing machine, and the Eiffel Tower.

■ Two lawyers were arguing a case in court and began to call each other names.

"You're a loop-brained shyster," roared one.

"And you're an ambulance chasing cockroach," roared the other.

The judge finally rapped for order. "Now that you two fellows have introduced each other to this court," he said, "you may proceed with the case."

- "Here's a letter from your father. The letterhead identifies him as an undertaker."

   "That's right, dear," he said. "What did you think he was?"
   "Didn't you tell me some time ago that he was a doctor?"
   "Oh, no. I never said that."
   "But I'm positive you did."
   "No, dear, you misunderstood. All I said was that he followed the medical profession."

Illustration

- A physician, who was asked the difference between rheumatism and gout, answered: "If you take a vice, put a finger between, and turn until you can't stand it any longer, that's rheumatism; if you turn once more, that's gout."

Income Tax

- Income taxes often transform nest eggs into goose eggs.

- A fool and his money are soon parted. The rest of us wait for tax time.

- The person who figured out the $2,000 exemption for a child must have been single.

- The president of a large manufacturing company was experiencing some minor difficulty with the Internal Revenue Service. His case had received up-to-the-minute publicity. Upon being introduced to a local service club, the chairperson began: "Our speaker this afternoon needs no introduction, but he could use a good tax attorney."

- Taxes are just like golf...you drive your heart out for the green, and then end up in the hole.

- The government crackdown on expense accounts may have one beneficial effect—it may bring back home cooking.

- *Irate wife* (in throes of washing and ironing, to husband filling in tax return): "Don't you *dare* list me as a dependent!"

  —Syd Hoff

- "He's the kind of an accountant you've got to admire. Last year he deducted eighty cartons of cigarettes from my income tax. Called it loss by fire!"

- Sign over door in tax office: *Watch Your Step*. As one leaves he will see written on the back of the same sign: *Watch Your Language*.

- The worker was handed a pay envelope which, through error, contained a blank check.

  The astonished fellow looked at it and moaned: "I knew it would happen eventually! My deductions have at last caught up with my salary!"

- On his income tax return the citizen neglected to mention a car he won in a raffle. But the Bureau of Internal Revenue knew.

  "Sir", the Bureau wrote, "the new car you omitted puts you in the 60 per cent tax bracket. Kindly remit."

  In reply the citizen wrote: "As payment of the 60 per cent due you on my new car I am sending four wheels, four doors, battery, radio, heater, and a fan belt—by express collect."

Inflation

- Billy walked into a drug store, laid a quarter on the counter, and asked for an ice cream cone.

  "Cones are forty cents," the clerk behind the counter informed him.

  "Then give me a package of chewing gum," said Billy.

  "Sorry, gum is forty-five cents."

  With that Billy walked away leaving the quarter on the counter.

  "You forgot your quarter," the clerk called out to him.

  "You keep it—it won't buy anything anyway," was little Billy's reply.

Ingenuity

- A Hollywood photographer puts vanity to work in collecting overdue bills from famed patrons. With his past-due notice he encloses an unretouched proof of the customer and requests permission to exhibit it in his studio window as a sample of his work. The patron usually shows up next day, cash in hand.

■ A shop was giving away toy balloons to children. One little fellow asked if he might have two. "Sorry," said the clerk, "but we give only one balloon to each boy. Have you a brother at home?"

The youngster was truthful, but he did want another balloon.

"No," he replied regretfully, then added hopefully, "but my sister has, and I want one for him."

■ An Iowa business, Mapmakers, Inc., needed $75,000 to work through a major cash flow process. Rather than seeking customary financing, the owner purchased a $900 want ad in the *Des Moines Register* declaring his need. The want ad read:

OUR NEED IS IMMEDIATE. IF YOU CAN HELP, PLEASE CALL...IMMEDIATELY

Within a few days, the business received an onslaught of support. One problem. The support was in the form of advice and good wishes—but, unfortunately, no money.

■ Having tried in vain to prevent youngsters smearing their shop windows on Halloween, the merchants of Itasca, Illinois, some years ago offered prizes for the best pictures drawn on the windows with soap. The plan not only curbed mischief, but uncovered talent. Crowds viewed the windows as if they constituted an art exhibition. One year the townspeople were so impressed with the beauty of two of the soap paintings that they sent the young artists to art school.

■ At a state banquet given by Frederick the Great of Prussia to his courtiers and noblemen, the monarch asked those present to explain why his revenues continued to diminish despite incoming taxes. An old general of the Hussars remarked dryly, "I will show Your Majesty what happens to the money." Procuring a piece of ice, he lifted it high for inspection; then he handed it to his neighbor and requested it be passed from hand to hand to the King. By the time it reached Frederick, it was about the size of a pea.

■ A gentleman went into a Paris barbershop with a small boy one day and explained that since he had an appointment in the neighborhood he would like his own hair cut first. This accomplished, he handed the small boy up into a chair, urged patience upon him, and departed. When the boy's haircut was finished, the gentleman had not returned, and the barber transferred the boy to an ordinary chair. A half hour passed.

"Don't worry," said the barber reassuringly. "I'm sure your father will be back soon." The boy looked startled. "He isn't my father" he said. "He just came up to me in the street and said, 'Come along, let's both get a haircut.'"

- With presses set to run off three million copies of Theodore Roosevelt's 1912 convention speech, the publisher found that permission had not been obtained to use photos of Roosevelt and his running mate, Governor Hiram Johnson, of California. Copyright law put the penalty for such oversights at $1 per copy.

  The chairman of the campaign committee was equal to the situation. He dictated a telegram to the Chicago studio that had taken the pictures: "Planning to issue three million copies Roosevelt speech with pictures Roosevelt and Johnson on cover. Great publicity opportunity for photographers. What will you pay us to use your photographs?"

  An hour later the reply was back: "Appreciate opportunity, but can pay only $250."

Installment Purchase

- Give a person credit for anything these days and he'll buy it.

- Buying on the installment plan makes the months shorter and the years longer.

- *Irate customer to credit manager*: "But you people were the ones who said the payments would be easy!"

- Show me a person who stands on their own two feet and I'll show you someone whose car has been repossessed.

- "Drive-in banks were established," the father explained to his son, "so that the cars could see their real owners!"

- *Item in gift shop*:
  "For the Man Who Has Everything: a calendar to remind him when the payments are due."

■ A man walked into a credit manager's office to pay the final installment on a baby carriage. The credit manager said, "Thank you, and how's the baby today?"

"Oh, I'm fine, thanks," replied the man.

■ Two men were discussing automobiles. "Yes, sir," said one, "I believe the best economy is to trade every two years. That's what I've done. And do you know," he continued proudly, "I haven't missed a payment in fourteen years."

Instruction—Instructions

■ When everything else fails—read the instructions.

■ The editor of a poultry journal received the following inquiry from a woman reader: "How long should a hen remain on the eggs?"

The editor replied: "Three weeks for chickens and four weeks for ducks."

A little later, the editor received a second letter: "Thank you for your kind advice," it read. "The hen remained on the eggs three weeks, and there were no chicks hatched. As I didn't care for ducks, I took her off the nest and sold the eggs."

■ A school teacher noticed one of her first graders leaning back in his chair, shirt unbuttoned, pants pulled low, and stomach exposed.

"What's wrong, Bobby?" she asked. "Why are you showing us your tummy?"

"Principal told me to," Bobby explained.

"The principal! Are you sure?"

"Yes, ma'am. Before school. When I told him my stomach was hurting."

The principal had advised Bobby to *stick it out* until noon.

Insurance

■ A man, nabbed by police while looting a jewelry store in a Western town, told the judge he was an insurance specialist.

"If nobody had any losses," he explained, "where would the insurance industry be?"

■ Some weeks after receiving a $1,200 check for the loss of her jewelry, an elderly woman informed her insurance company that she had found the missing property in her cupboard.

"I didn't think it would be fair to keep both the jewels and the money, so I think you will be pleased to know that I sent the $1,200 to the Red Cross."

Insurance, Fire

- A man bought several boxes of cigars and had them insured against fire. When he had smoked them, he put in a claim against the insurance company that they had been destroyed by fire.

  The company refused to pay, and the man sued. The judge ruled that the company had given the man a policy protecting against fire, and must pay.

  As soon as the man accepted the money, the company had him arrested on a charge of arson.

Insurance, Life

- A life insurance salesperson was standing beside a tractor trying to sell a farmer a policy, but the farmer, looking down, said, "No, sir, I want no life insurance—when I die I want it to be a sad day for everybody."

- *Mr. Jones*: "I have enough life insurance. Don't need any more."

  Insurance salesperson: "How much do you carry?"

  Mr. Jones: "$7,500 double indemnity."

  Insurance salesperson: "You don't intend to stay dead very long, do you, Mr. Jones?"

- A man went into an insurance office to have his life insured.

  "Ride a bicycle?" the agent asked.

  "No," answered the man.

  "Drive a car?"

  "No."

  "Perhaps you fly?"

  "No, no," said the applicant. "Nothing dangerous—"

  The agent cut in. "Sorry, sir," he said, "but we no longer insure pedestrians."

Integrity

- An elderly lady rented a room to two boys whom she did not know, and she worried some at first but soon she stopped fretting. She discovered, so she told a neighbor, that they were nice boys. "They must be nice," she explained to her friend, "because they have towels from the YMCA."

- A successful businessperson was talking to her competitor. "I said it before and I'll say it again," she declaimed. "There may be many, many ways of making money, but there's only one honest one."

  "What's that?" the competitor asked.

  "Just as I suspected," crowed the businessperson. "You don't know!"

- "Will you hold my horse for a few minutes?" a farmer asked a well-dressed stranger.

  "Sir," said the stranger, "I'll have you know that I'm a member of Congress."

  "Oh, that's all right," said the farmer, "I'll trust you anyway."

- A client went to his attorney and said: "I am going into a business deal with a man I do not trust. I want you to frame an air-tight contract which he can't break and which will protect me from any sort of mischief which he may have in his mind."

  "Listen, my friend," said the attorney, "there is no group of words in the English language which will take the place of plain honesty between men, or which will fully protect either of you if you plan to deceive each other."

  —*Ernest Haycock*

- Probably no man had a longer or more distinguished career in sports than the veteran coach, Amos Alonzo Stagg, for forty-two years the idol of students and graduates of the University of Chicago. Yet he was more admired for his rugged character and uncompromising honesty.

  Stagg's championship baseball team was defending its college title. The batter had singled, and one of Stagg's men was racing home with the winning run. Stagg shouted, "Get back to third base. You cut it by a yard." "But the umpire didn't see it," the runner protested. "That doesn't make any difference," roared Stagg. "Get back!"

  It cost the game but a character battle was won.

- When he was 24 years old, Abraham Lincoln served as the post-master of New Salem, Illinois, for which he was paid an annual salary of $55.70.

Even then, 24 years before he entered the White House, the rail splitter was showing the character that earned him the title of "Honest Abe."

The New Salem post office was closed in 1836, but it was several years before an agent arrived from Washington to settle accounts with ex-postmaster Lincoln, who was a struggling lawyer not doing very well.

The agent informed him that $17 was due the government. Lincoln crossed the room, opened an old trunk and took out a yellow cotton rag, bound with a string.

Untying it, he spread out the cloth and there was the $17. He had been holding it untouched for all the years.

"I never use anyone's money but my own," he said.

Interruption—Interruptions

■ An advertising director went to discuss a TV show with a well-known actor. The actor apologized for the absence of his wife, explaining that she was upstairs looking after their five children.

"What are their ages?"

"Five, four, three, two and one," smiled the actor.

"Say," commented the advertising executive, "I hope I'm not keeping you!"

—Robin Goodfellow

Investing

■ From jewelry to furniture, Warren Buffet's investments are considered savvy and safe. His conservative and long-term strategy of buying undervalued stock has earned Buffet a highly regarded reputation as an investor. In addition, this investment process has made Warren Buffet one of the richest people in the world. However, he attributes his success to two simple rules: "The first rule is not to lose money. The second rule is not to forget the first rule."

■ Although a prolific writer, the French philosopher, Voltaire, achieved financial independence by age 40 through more creative means. Voltaire invested his earnings in young nobility awaiting their massive inheritance. He loaned them money at 10 percent interest for life—based on their future fortunes. Anxious to obtain the cash, young people eagerly negotiated the loans with little thought about the long years of payment ahead. Voltaire died a rich man at 82, outliving the projections of many.

- *FORBES* magazine's driving force and financial genius, B.C. Forbes, received a letter from his friend, Will Rogers, commenting on Forbes' stock advice column. Rogers wrote, " I hope some day, brother Forbes, to be rich enough to be able to act on some of your stock market advice." Initially, Forbes was flattered by the compliment. Later, after rereading the letter several times, Forbes wasn't sure it was meant to be a compliment.

J

Joint Effort

- A flea and an elephant walked side by side over a little bridge. Said the flea to the elephant, after they had crossed: "Boy, we sure did shake that thing."

- A burglar who had entered a poor minister's house at midnight was disturbed by the awakening of the occupant of the room. Drawing his knife, he said:
  "If you stir, you are a dead man. I'm hunting for money."
  "Let me get up and strike a light," said the minister, "and I'll hunt with you."

- The organist was giving a brilliant concert in a famous old church. As he reached the intermission, he stepped to the back of the organ for a bit of rest. There he found an oldish gentleman smoking his pipe as he rested from the chore of pumping air for the big organ. The fellow smiled and commented: "We're giving them quite a concert, aren't we?"
  The genius responded tartly, "What do you mean 'we' old man? I'm giving the concert!"
  He went out front. In came the audience. The organist struck a pose with hands raised, then let them descend for the opening of the next number. There was no sound. He dashed behind the organ. There was the man, puffing his pipe. The light dawned on

the genius and with a smile he admitted: "You are right, we are giving them a concert."

Journalism

■ The city editor had just been informed that a wire had fallen across Main Street in a storm. He assigned two reporters to the story.

"No one knows whether the wire is live or not," he said. "So one of you is to touch it, and the other is to write the story."

■ "Dad," said the subscriber's little daughter, "I know why editors call themselves 'we.'"

"Why"

"So the person who doesn't like what's printed will think there are too many for him to lick."

■ "What was your business before you were captured by my men?" asked the cannibal chief.

"I was assistant editor of a newspaper," answered the captive.

"In that case, young man, you can cheer up'" said the chief. "Promotion awaits you. After dinner you'll be editor-in-chief."

■ "What do you mean," roared the politician, "by publicly insulting me in your rag of a paper? I will not stand for it, and I demand an immediate apology."

"Just a moment," answered the editor. "Didn't the news appear exactly as you gave it to us; namely, that you had resigned as city treasurer?"

"It did, but where did you put it?—in the column under the heading public improvements."

■ A man rushed into the newspaper office and demanded to see the editor. "Sir," he cried, as he strode up and down the room, "your paper has libeled me. You have called me the lightweight champion."

"But that is true," returned the editor. "You are Mr. Fightwell, aren't you?"

"Yes, yes," cried the other, "but it's my brother who is the boxer. I'm the coal merchant."

■ A newspaper reporter was sent to cover a disastrous flood which had just wiped out a central Pennsylvania town.

After viewing the scene, the reporter went to the telegraph office and filed his story, which started out as follows:

"God is sitting on the hills of this little Pennsylvania town tonight..."

The hard-boiled telegraph editor read the first line and promptly sent back the following message:

"Rush interview with God."

■ The editor of the local newspaper queried the new applicant for the job of rewrite person. Said the editor, "Are you any good?"

"Sure," was the reply.

"All right, then, fix this and cut it short," instructed the editor, handing him the Ten Commandments.

The applicant gave the copy a glance, seemed a little nonplussed, then stepped over to the desk and wrote briefly, and handed it to the editor who studied the paper for only a moment, then looked up and said, "You're hired."

The rewrite on the paper was, "Don't."

Judge—Judges

■ There was a certain judge sitting in a courtroom with two lawyers, and one of the lawyers got mad at the other over an argument and suddenly turning upon him said, "Of all the unmitigated, consummate asses that ever lived, you are the absolute limit!"

The judge rapped heavily with his gavel and cried: "Gentlemen, you forget that I am present."

■ A city lawyer was trying a case before a justice of the peace in a rural community. After long discussion over a certain point, the justice ruled against the lawyer who thereupon rose, and began: "If Your Honor please—"

"Stop right there, young man. You might just as well sit down. I've already made up my mind, and I never change it. I know law and I don't need nobody to tell me nothin'. I'm right, I know it and there's nothin' else to it."

"Why, Your Honor," said the lawyer, "of course you are right. I merely wanted to show you what a big fool Blackstone was."

Jurisdiction

■ Asked to officiate at a friend's wedding ceremony, Justice Felix Frankfurter explained that he did not have the authority to perform the ceremony.

"What!" exclaimed his friend "A Supreme Court Justice doesn't have the authority to marry people! How come?"

"I guess," replied Frankfurter, "it is because marriage is not considered a federal offense."

Justice

■ A farmer was a witness in a a hog-stealing case and seemed to be stretching a point in favor of the accused.

"Do you," roared the prosecuting attorney, "know the nature of the oath?"

"Sure," said the farmer.

"Do you know," demanded the attorney, "that you are not to bear false witness against your neighbor?"

"I'm not bearing false witness against him!" returned the farmer indignantly. "I'm bearing it for him!"

K

Know-How

■ A man in Alaska was arrested for bigamy. It was discovered that he had a wife in Nome, another wife in Fairbanks, and a third in Juneau. The judge looked down at the culprit and sternly asked: "How could you do such a thing?"

The bigamist replied: "Fast dog team."

L

Law—Laws

■ *The Court*: "Why do you wish a new trial for your client?"

Lawyer: "On the grounds of newly-discovered matter, your honor."

The Court: "And what's the nature of that?"

Lawyer: "My client has dug up $500 that I didn't know he had."

- It was during the impaneling of a jury that the following colloquy occurred:
    "You are a property holder?"
    "Yes, your honor."
    "Married or single?"
    "I have been married five years, your honor."
    "Have you formed or expressed any opinion?"
    "Not for five years, your honor."

- A young lawyer was defending an old convict on a charge of burglary in a state where the court rules allow each side one hour to address the jury. The young lawyer, somewhat nervous, consulted a veteran member of the bar who happened to be standing near. "How much time do you think I should take in addressing the jury?" he asked in a rather pompous manner.
    "Take the full hour," was the gruff reply.
    "The full hour? I'd intended taking only fifteen minutes."
    "Take the full hour," repeated the old lawyer.
    "But why?"
    "Because the longer you talk, the longer you will keep your client out of jail."

- A little boy was brought before a magistrate and charged with throwing stones at passing railway trains.
    "What have you to say?" asked the stern-faced judge.
    "I didn't throw no stones, sir, I was only going to," said the boy.
    "Only going to!" echoed the magistrate. "Well, the intent was there, and as a deterrent I shall fine you $5."
    The father took the youngster by the hand and proceeded to leave the courtroom when the judge called him back and reminded him that he had failed to pay the fine.
    "That's quite so," replied the parent. "I should have done so; but as the intent is just as good as the deed in the eyes of the law, you're paid."

- During a moot court argument at the Harvard Law School, one pair of students was given a case rather equally divided on the issues. It so happened that about a week before the oral argument, however, an advance sheet came out with an almost identical case in a highly considered jurisdiction. The decision was squarely for the defendant. Student counsel for the plaintiff felt lost and sure enough his opponent made effective use of the case in point. When it came the plaintiff's turn to argue, the first thing the judge said was, "Counsel, what about this new case which defendant has cited?"

Without a moment's hesitation, the attorney for the plaintiff replied: "Your Honor, these cases are easily distinguishable—why, even the names are different!"

Lawyer—Lawyers

- "Moses was a great lawgiver," said Uncle Eben. "But de way he was satisfied to keep de ten commandments short an' to de point shows he wasn't no regular lawyer."

- "Do you have a criminal lawyer in town?" a tourist asked an old-timer.

  "Well, we think so," the old man replied, "but we can't prove it."

- My wife, a lawyer, often refuses to accompany me to parties because so many people spoil her evening by asking her for advice. I asked a doctor if this happened to him. "All the time!" he said.

  "Then how do you get rid of these people?"

  "I have a wonderful remedy," the doctor grinned. "When someone begins telling me his ailments, I stop him with one word, 'Undress!'"

- A well-known lawyer had just finished an important case which he had lost. He was upset and worried and, unable to sleep, he went wandering through the train on which he was a passenger.

  By mistake he got into a car that had been reserved for mental patients, just as the man in white was checking up on his charges.

  "One, two, three, four, five," the man counted, and then he spotted the unfamiliar face of the lawyer. "Who are you?" the attendant asked.

  "I'm a lawyer," he answered with sheepish pride.

  The male nurse nodded his head with understanding and continued counting "...six, seven, eight, nine..."

- Professor of Law Samuel Siegel helped would-be attorneys understand how to tackle difficult cases. "When you're presenting a case, if you have the facts on your side, hammer the facts," Siegel advised. "If you have the law on your side, then hammer the law."

  "What if you don't have the facts or the law," a student asked, "then what do you do?"

  "Well, in that case," responded Siegel, "hammer on the table."

- A minister, a doctor, and a lawyer, adrift on a raft, sighted a distant island. There were signs of human habitation, but no persons in view.

  Since the drift was away from the island, the lawyer volunteered to swim ashore and bring help. Just as he was about to dive into the sea, the minister urged a word of parting prayer, so a brief religious service was held.

  Eagerly the two remaining voyagers watched their companion. Presently they were horrified to see a huge shark making directly for the lawyer. At the last moment, however, the shark veered away and the swimmer was saved. Later, another shark came into view and he, too, veered sharply away when he came close to the struggling man.

  "There!" said the minister triumphantly. "Observe an answer to our prayers. Because of that service we held, the Lord has preserved our friend from the hungry sharks."

  "Well, that may be," the doctor said dubiously, "but personally I'm inclined to think of it as a professional courtesy."

Lawyer—Client

- *Lawyer (calling on a client who is in prison cell)*: "What I'm looking for now is a judge with a terrific sense of humor."

- The late Lord Birkett, as defense counsel, had just secured the acquittal of a woman who had been accused of two murders. After the trial he threw his wig on the table and said to his junior, Mr. Ingle-Foot: "Cases of this kind take years off a man's life."

  "Perhaps," replied Mr. Foot, "but they add years to his client's."

- The man was facing trial and possible imprisonment. "I know the evidence is against me," he told his lawyer, "but I've got $50,000 in cash to fight this case."

"You'll never go to prison with that amount of money," the lawyer assured him.

He didn't. He went there broke.

■ An elderly man consulted a lawyer. He wanted to buy a piece of property but wanted a mortgage. The lawyer told him he needed a deed. The man insisted on a mortgage because his friend Olson had had a deed and the fellow with the mortgage came along and took his property away from him. So he wanted a mortgage!

■ A lawyer was drawing up papers of partenership for two manufacturers. He went over the papers before the final signing, but he found them incomplete.

"There is no mention here," he said, "of fire or bankruptcy. These must go in."

"Quite right," said the partners, speaking together, "put them in, but the profits are to be divided equally in both cases."

■ A man was charged with stealing a case of canned goods from the storeroom of a grocery store.

"Now," said his lawyer, "if I take your case you must tell me honestly. Did you or did you not steal those canned peaches?"

"Well, yes sir, I did," the man admitted.

"That's all right," replied the lawyer. "You give me half of them."

When the case came into court the lawyer addressed the jury thus:

"This man did not get any more of those peaches than I did."

The verdict was "not guilty."

■ The plaintiff in a damage suit had enjoyed very little education in his life and was wholly unused to court proceedings. He was considerably disturbed to see that the defendant corporation had two men from its legal staff on the case.

During the recess for lunch he turned to his own lawyer and said, "I ought to have a second lawyer on my side."

"What's the matter?" demanded the astonished counsel. "I think I am presenting your case very effectively. In fact, I don't see how we can lose."

The plaintiff stroked his chin reflectively. Then he explained, "I notice the corporation has two lawyers. When one of them is up speakin' for their side, the other is sittin' there thinkin'. When you're up speakin' for our side, there ain't nobody thinkin'."

Lazy—Laziness

■ The business owner carefully observed a new employee for the first thirty days of service with the company. Not being a real ball of fire, the employee displayed a less than enthusiastic work ethic. Unable to restrain herself any longer, the business owner screamed at the employee, "You're one of the laziest people I have ever seen. You have barely completed a week's worth of work since I hired you. Help me understand one reason why I should keep you around?"

The employee calmly pondered the question and then responded, "One benefit is that when I take a vacation, you won't need to find someone to fill in."

Leadership

■ Someone once asked a famous conductor of a great symphony orchestra which orchestral instrument he considered to be the most difficult to play. The conductor thought for a moment and then said: "Second fiddle. I can get plenty of first violinists. But to find one who can play second fiddle with enthusiasm—that's a problem. And if we have no second fiddles, we have no harmony!"

Losing

■ Homecoming was a disaster. The home team, celebrating their school's 50th homecoming football game, was easily defeated by a score of 73 to 14. The fans were unimpressed, the players were depressed, but the coach maintained his sense of humor. A reporter asked what he felt the turning point was. Coach hesitated a moment and then responded: "Somewhere between the time we left the locker room and the conclusion of the national anthem."

Loyalty

■ Serving as Vice President during Lyndon Johnson's Presidency, the late Hubert Humphrey was criticized for not speaking out when he disagreed with Johnson. However, Humphrey held his ground and remained loyal to the Texan President.

During one press conference, reporters challenged the Vice President by hurling controversial questions at him. Always the diplomat, Humphrey refrained from a terse "No comment" response. Rather, he faced each probing question with a smile and replied, "The eyes of Texas are upon me."

Luck

■ A group of theatrical people were trying to help a former star who had been persistently unlucky. Knowing that he was too proud to accept money as a gift they rigged up a bogus raffle.

They told him that they would all draw slips from a hat, and that the person who drew the number four would get $500. To make sure that the old actor would win, they wrote *four* on every slip.

After the drawing, the conspirators glanced at their slips, crumpled them up and waited for their friend to announce that he had the lucky number. But the old fellow never opened his mouth. Finally, unable to bear the suspense, they asked him what number he had drawn from the hat.

"Six and seven-eighths," he answered glumly.

■ A peddler of lottery tickets tried to sell a chance to Baron Rothschild, head of the famous European banking family.

"What would I want with a lottery ticket?" protested the annoyed Baron.

"Oh, come on," pleaded the peddler. "They're only fifty cents each. Go on, take a chance."

To get rid of the nuisance, Baron Rothschild bought the lottery ticket. The next day, bright and early, the peddler was on the Baron's doorstep. "You won the first prize!" he cried. "$300,000!"

"Well!" exclaimed the pleased Baron. "I suppose I ought to reward you." He thought a moment. "Which would you rather have?" he asked at last, "$12,000 in cash or $3,600 a year for the rest of your life?"

"Give me the $12,000," said the peddler. "With the kind of luck you Rothschilds have, I wouldn't live another six months."

M

Majority Rule

- In 1747, Mr. John Brown was invited to become the pastor of a church at Hingham. There was but one opponent to his settlement, a man whom Mr. Brown won over by a stroke of good humor. He asked for the grounds of his opposition. "I like your person and your manner," was the reply, "but your preaching, sir, I disapprove."

  "Then," said Mr. Brown, "we are agreed. I do not like my preaching very well myself, but how great a folly it is for you and me to set up our opinion against that of the whole parish."

- All the great injustices of history have been committed in the name of unchecked and unbridled "majority rule."

  The late Senator James A. Reed, of Missouri, in one of the most forceful speeches ever delivered before the Senate, observed with great truth: "The majority crucified Jesus Christ; the majority burned the Christians at the stake; the majority established slavery; the majority jeered when Columbus said the world was round; the majority threw him into a dungeon for having discovered a new world; the majority cut off the ears of John Pym because he dared advocate the liberty of the press."

Medical Profession, See also Doctor—Patient

- A nurse in the maternity ward asked a young medical student why he was so enthusiastic about obstetrics. He said sheepishly, "When I was on medical rotation I suffered from heart attacks, asthma, and itch. In surgery I was sure I had ulcers. In the psychiatric wards I was sure I was losing my mind. Now, in obstetrics I can relax."

- When asked by a young intern which medicine he considered the greatest boon, the old doctor looked back thoughtfully over a half century of practice. As memories crowded in upon him, they brought a clear, sharp recognition of the one medicine which he considered to be the master medicine of all. To the intern he said:

"The most wonderful medicine is not compounded of rare and expensive drugs; it is one of the most commonplace things. I know in fact, it is not a drug at all. You can spell the name of this master medicine with four simple letters, W-O-R-K."

■ A man of seventy-five won $20,000 in a sweepstakes. His family didn't want to tell him because he had a weak heart and they were in fear of what the shock might do to him. So they consulted the family physician who said he would take care of the situation and that they should leave the matter in his hands. The doctor approached the old man casually and asked him what he would do if he were lucky enough to win $20,000 in a sweepstakes. The old gent replied, "I'd give you half." With that the old doc himself keeled over and died.

■ In writing prescriptions physicians usually employ Latin terms. There are several reasons for this.

In the first place, it is a custom which has been followed since the time when medical science was in its infancy and medical people were wont to write what they had to say in Latin.

Secondly, the botanical names of plants are usually in Latin, (1) because scientific experts give them their names, and (2) because often the English name for a plant in one part of the country has an entirely different meaning in another.

It is frequently advisable that a patient be kept in ignorance of the character of the drug they are taking lest they attempt to use it without a physician's advice on another occasion, and thereby do themself injury.

—Dr. M.S. Young

■ Dr. William Osler, having been invited to inspect a famous London hospital, was proudly shown about by several physicians and surgeons. Finally the charts were reached, and he looked them over carefully, observing the system of abbreviations: SF for Scarlet Fever, TB for Tuberculosis, D for Diphtheria, and so on. All the diseases seemed to be pretty well under control except for one indicated by the symbol GOK.

"I observe," said the famous doctor, "that you have a sweeping epidemic of GOK on your hands. This is a symbol not in common use in American medical circles; just what is GOK?"

"Oh!" one of his hosts lightly replied, "When we can't diagnose, God Only Knows."

—*Walter Neale*

■ A doctor had trouble with his plumbing. The pipes in his bathroom began to leak. The leak became bigger and bigger.

Even though it was 2 a.m. the doctor decided to phone his plumber. Naturally the plumber became angry at being awakened at that hour of the morning. "For Pete's sake, Doc," he wailed, "this is some time to wake up a guy."

"Well," the doctor answered testily, "you've never hesitated to call me in the middle of the night with a medical problem. Now it just happens I've got a plumbing emergency."

There was a moment's silence. Then the plumber spoke up. "Right you are, Doc," he agreed, "Tell me what's wrong."

The doctor explained about the leak in the bathroom.

"Tell you what to do," the plumber offered. "Take two aspirins every four hours, drop them down the pipe. If the leak hasn't cleared up by morning, phone me at the office."

Millinery

■ *Mrs. Brown*: "Whenever I'm down in the dumps, I get myself a new hat."

Mrs. Jones: "I've often wondered where you got them."

Mistake—Mistakes

■ A professional carpet layer stepped back to admire his customary flawless work. While surveying the installed carpet, he reached into his shirt pocket for a cigarette and realized that his pack of cigarettes was missing. At the same time, he noticed that there was a lump under the carpet, about the size of a cigarette package. Frustrated with his carelessness, the carpet layer realized that he was in a predicament. There was no way to retrieve his cigarette package from under the attached carpet. Finally, he decided to beat the object flat, thereby destroying any evidence of his mistake.

Satisfied with the outcome, he picked up his tools and began loading the truck. He couldn't believe his eyes. Laying on the seat of his truck was the mislaid pack of cigarettes. "But what about...?" It was then that the homeowner's voice broke his disbelief.

"Hey, have you seen my son's gerbil?"

- Doctors can bury their mistakes, but architects can only advise their clients to plant ivy.

- A famous department store decided to honor its two-millionth customer. She was welcomed by the store president, interviewed on the radio, and loaded down with many packages of choice merchandise.

  She then proceeded to her original destination—the complaint desk.

- A worker was shorted two dollars in his pay envelope, and complained to the accountant.

  "You were overpaid twenty dollars last week and didn't object," reasoned the accountant.

  "I know," said the employee. "I don't mind overlooking one mistake, but when it happens the second time, I think it's time to complain."

Modern Age

- A business firm wrote to another corporation saying, "Our electronic brain had computed that the cost of the work you want done will be..."

  The following reply was received a few days later:

  "As this is more than we anticipated, we would like to suggest that your electronic brain make an appointment with our electronic brain to discuss ways and means of reducing the cost of work."

N

Negotiation

- "Larry King Live" featured New York's real estate baron Donald Trump. The interview had just begun when Trump said, "Do you mind if I sit back a little? Because your breath is very bad. It really is. Has this been told to you before?"

  Taken back, King responded, "No."

Trump continued, "Okay, then I won't bother."

"So that's how you get the edge," commented the composed King. "See, it's that little thing you threw me right then that no one has ever told me."

"Nobody told you that? You're kidding?" Trump questioned.

"Nobody."

"Okay, Larry," Trump relented, "your breath is great."

Was the whole thing staged? Were Trump's comments intended to shake the unshakeable Larry King? King's producers explained the event as a demonstration of Trump's ability to get the edge in negotiations.

Newspaper—Newspapers

■ The following correction appeared in a small town newspaper:

"Our paper carried the notice last week that Mr. John Jones is a defective on the police force. This was a typographical error. Mr. Jones is really a detective on the police farce."

O

Opportunity

■ Temptations, unlike opportunities, will always give you many second chances.

—*O.A. Battista*

P

Parent—Child

■ A young businessperson returned home late, tired from a hard day at the office, to find her two children rushing madly about the house. She scolded them both and sent them to bed. The next morning she found this note pinned to her bedroom door:

"Be good to your children and they will be good to you. Yours truly, God."

Partnership

- Two brothers in the retail coal business had an intricate problem. One of them had taken an interest in the history and theory of ethics.

  "It's a fine thing for you to study ethics," the first brother said, "but if I study ethics too, who's gonna weigh the coal?"

- The high-pressure salesperson was giving a pitch to a small manufacturer. "I'm the best in the business," he boasted. "Put me to work for you and you'll really go places!"

  "That may be so," said the tired, overworked owner, "but anybody I hire has to start at the bottom. First you gotta be my partner."

- A small businessperson and her partner closed their office at noon one Saturday and went to the movies. After they had been seated, one of them nudged the other and gasped, "Gosh, we forgot to close the safe!"

  "What's the difference?" asked the other. "We're both here, aren't we?"

- A twenty-year business partnership enjoyed by Sam and Pete ended very abruptly when Sam had to take a week off after catching a virus. On the third day of Sam's indisposition, Pete phoned from the office and said in an excited voice:

  "There's $5,000 missing from the safe, Sam. What shall I do?"

  "Put it back," Sam ordered coldly.

- A tramp knocked on the door of the inn known as *George and the Dragon*. The owner opened the door, and the tramp asked, "Could you spare a hungry man a bite to eat?"

  "No!" replied the woman, slamming the door in his face.

  A few minutes later the tramp knocked again. The owner came to the door again. This time the tramp asked, "Could I have a few words with George?"

- A story of mid-nineteenth century tells of the man who, upon meeting a friend, told him he was going into business.

  "What sort of business?" the friend asked.

  "A partnership," the other replied.

"Are you putting in much capital?"

"No. I put in no capital. I put in the experience."

"And he puts in the capital, is that it?"

"Yes, we go into business for three years. He puts in the capital and I put in the experience. At the end of three years I will have the capital; and he will have the experience."

■ We've just heard about the West Coast dress buyer who dropped in at the New York firm of Jackson, Parker, and Lewis. "Mr. Jackson or Mr. Parker," he requested.

"Sorry," said the receptionist, "they're both out of town."

"Mr. Lewis, then."

"Mr. Lewis is tied up."

The next day he returned and was again unsuccessful. On the third day he telephoned and was told the two partners were still out of town.

"And Mr. Lewis?"

"Sorry, he's tied up."

"What goes on?" the buyer shouted. "He's been tied up for three days!"

"Oh," explained the receptionist. "Mr. Lewis is the junior partner. When the others go away, they *always* tie him up."

People

■ A wise man of the Orient once remarked: "There are three kinds of people in all types of organizations—rowboat people, sailboat people, and steamboat people. Rowboat people need to be pushed or shoved along. Sailboat people move when a favorable wind is blowing. Steamboat people move continuously, through calm or storm. They usually are masters of themselves, their surroundings, and their fate."

Perfection

■ Benjamin Franklin is regarded as the leading printer the United States has produced. He was also the country's first outstanding salesperson!

A competitor by the name of Andrew Bradford had the contract to do all the public printing for the State of Pennsylvania. The governor made an important address. Bradford printed it in his usual slovenly manner. This presented the opportunity Franklin wanted. He reprinted the speech elegantly in a form appropriate to the governor's office. Then he mailed a copy with his compliments to the governor and to each member of the Assembly. The next year he was awarded the contract for all the public printing.

- Years ago, when the Dow Chemical Company was just getting started, Herbert H. Dow, the founder, stood talking with the head of the electrical shops when a stranger walked up to them, stating that he was an electrician and had heard there might be an opening. He went on at great length about his qualifications, repeatedly emphasizing that he never, never made a mistake.

  Before the head of the electrical shops could say a word, Dow spoke up. "Sorry, mister. But I've got 3,000 people working at the plant, and they make at least 3,000 mistakes a day. It wouldn't do at all to hire someone who never makes a mistake!"

  —*Pete Derrio*

Point of View

- A parishioner called at the minister's home. Presently the minister's little son went up to the visiting lady and blurted, "My, how ugly you are."

  Horrified, his mother remonstrated, "Johnny! Whatever can you mean by saying such a thing?"

  "I only meant—meant it for a joke, mother," Johnny stammered.

  "Well," his mother purred unwittingly, "how much better the joke would have been if you had said to Mrs. Smith, 'How pretty you are!'"

- In a certain city council of Sweden, the two political parties are about equally divided. At one time, it is related, the peasant member from Upsala made a bitter speech against his adversaries, the Communists, and terminated his address with this remark:

  "Half of the members of this assembly are idiots."

  Inevitably, there was an uproar of protests. The farmer was obliged to make a written apology. That same night, he posted the following declaration on the door of the city hall:

  "I wish to assert that half the members of the municipal council are not idiots."

Policy

- The Nordstrom company is a specialty retailer based in the Seattle area. Along with their commitment to quality services for customers (including on-the-spot gift-wrapping), is a belief that policies should be kept short and sweet. In fact, Nordstrom's managers function with a one-sentence policy manual: "Use your best judgment at all times."

Professional Fees

- The difference between an itch and an allergy is about $50.00.

- Some doctors tell their patients the worst—others just mail the bill.

- The only thing the modern obstetrician has in common with the stork is the size of his bill.

- You go to the psychiatrist when you're slightly cracked and keep going until you're completely broke.

- *Hospital patient receiving the bill for an operation*: "No wonder they wore masks in the operating room."

- Nowadays one needs two anesthetics for an operation: one to put you to sleep and the other when you get the surgeon's bill.

- *Patient*: "How can I ever repay you for all you've done for me?"
  Doctor: "By check, money order, or cash."

- A pastor at a small church prayed for the Lord to keep him humble and poor. One of the deacons turned to his neighbor and said, "If the Lord will keep him humble, we will do the rest."

- An attempt was once made to lure Professor Louis Agassiz, the noted scientist and naturalist, into delivering a lecture by promising him a fat fee. He replied: "I cannot afford to waste my time in making money."

- The surgeon prescribed a simple operation to relieve his patient's ailment. Asked if he wanted the operation performed immediately, the patient replied, "How will it affect my hobby?"
  Puzzled, the doctor inquired, "And what is your hobby?"
  "Saving money," was the reply.

- The woman was choking on a chicken bone. A friend called for a doctor who removed it. "What do I owe you?" asked the woman. "At least half of what you were ready to pay when the bone was still in your throat," replied the doctor.

- Igor Stravinsky was offered $4,000 to compose the music for a Hollywood film.

  "It is not enough," he said.

  "It's what we paid your predecessor," the producer said.

  "My predecessor had talent," Stravinsky replied. "I have not. So for me the work is more difficult."

- Fritz Kreisler, the violin virtuoso, was invited to dinner by a New York dowager and asked to bring his violin. At the end of dinner he was asked if he would play for the guests. Kreisler obliged. The next day the dowager was amazed to receive a bill for $5,000 from the artist.

  "But Mr. Kreisler," she protested by phone, "you were my guest."

  "No," Kreisler replied, "I was your performer. Had I been your guest, you would have invited Mrs. Kreisler."

- After giving the new patient a thorough diagnostic examination and prescribing medicines and special foods, the Park Avenue doctor announced that his fee would be $300.

  The visitor blanched. "That's almost as much as I make in a week."

  The doctor offered to reduce the bill to $200. Still the man protested.

  After much haggling, the M.D. reluctantly accepted $100. "But why," he asked, "did you come to a specialist like me? Why not a charity clinic? That wouldn't cost you anything."

  "Oh, no. When I'm sick, money's no object."

Profit—Profits

- When a store sells you something for a dollar, the article you bought cost the merchant 61 cents on the average. That leaves 39 cents to be accounted for. And a good many people believe that this is all profit. If that were true, merchandising would be a gold mine—but it isn't.

The 39 cents is called markup, which means the difference between the price a retailer pays and the price at which he offers it for sale. The expenses in operating the store must come out of the markup. These include payroll costs (which usually account for more than half the markup), rent, utilities, advertising, insurance, losses—and, of course, taxes.

How much of that markup , then, sticks in the merchant's pockets in the form of profit? The answer, based on exhaustive factual surveys, is 1.9 cents. In other words, less than 2 cents out of every dollar of sales is left to the retailer, stockholders, or investors after all the bills are met.

The consumer has a pretty high stake in everything that runs up the cost of retail business. Higher taxes, higher wages, must mean higher costs since the retailer, to remain in business, cannot take them out of what is left. It all adds up.

■ A young man immigrated to the United States with a dream of being successful, the clothes on his back, and his new bride. He opened a roadside vegetable stand which turned into a full-fledged grocery store. Then a second store was opened, and a third, and a fourth. The man became quite wealthy and his family enjoyed a lifestyle he never thought possible.

One day, the grocery magnate's son visited his dad at work. He had just graduated from college in Business Management and was considering joining his father in the grocery business. The son was amused at his father's ancient accounting procedures. All receipts were put in a cardboard box and bills to be paid in another box. That was it! No calculator, cash register, or computer to insure accuracy. "How in the world, Dad, do you know what your profits are?" the astonished son asked.

"Dear boy," began his father, "it is really quite simple." Pointing to the box with the cash he continued, "I have always kept an accurate count of this money. Then I add in the cost of our beautiful home, my car, your mother's car, your car, our summer home on the lake, and your expensive college education. Subtract the clothes I had on my back when we arrived in the U.S. and that's the profit."

Property Owner—Tenant

■ A party of tourists was making a tour through the ancient castle. "For centuries," explained their guide proudly, "nothing here has been changed. No brick has been laid, not a tile replaced, none of the walls redecorated, and even the floorboards are the original ones."

"Fancy that!" whispered one woman to her husband. "Apparently they have here the same owner we have!"

■ *Owner to prospective tenant:* "You know we keep it very quiet and orderly here. Do you have children?"

"No."

"A piano, television, or phonograph?"

"No."

"Do you have a dog, cat, or parrot?"

"No, but my fountain pen scratches a little sometimes."

■ He got out of bed at 2 A.M. He threw a dressing gown over his pajamas and galloped down two flights of stairs to the apartment manager's flat. He rapped sharply. No answer. He knocked again, and again. Finally the door opened. A sleepy-eyed landlord yelled, "Well, what do you want?"

The tenant took a deep breath. "I just want to inform you," he said, "that I won't be able to pay the rent this month."

"Is that why you woke me in the middle of the night?" the manager howled. "Couldn't you tell me that in the morning just as well?"

"Certainly," admitted the tenant, "but why should I be worrying alone?"

■ When John Barrymore scored his first hit on Broadway, he took an apartment in New York's Greenwich Village and spent his newly found wealth buying furnishings for it. He even built a garden on the roof. To accomplish this, tons of earth had to be hauled up.

Soon after the garden had been completed, it belatedly came to the attention of the owner of the building.

"What have you done?" he wailed to the actor. "This roof cannot sustain such a weight. It will collapse!"

"Are you sure?" said Barrymore.

"Of course I'm sure. Now what are you going to do about it?"

"I'm going to move, of course!" retorted Barrymore. "You don't expect me to live in an unsafe building, do you?"

Psychiatry

- The latest thing in shock treatment is a psychiatrist who sends the bills in advance.

- "I used to be terribly conceited," a Hollywood chap confided, "but my psychiatrist straightened me out and now I'm one of the nicest guys in town."

- Psychiatrists charge $75 an hour. Everyone goes—they say it does wonders. Let's be honest: if you were to lie down an hour a day, you'd feel better, too.

- *Psychiatrist*: "Congratulations. You're cured."
  Patient: "Some cure. Before I came to you, I was Napoleon. Now I'm just another nobody."

- A psychiatrist saw another psychiatrist plodding down the street carrying a couch on his head.
  "Why the couch?" she called after her colleague.
  "House call," replied the burdened one.

- A woman walked into a psychiatrist's office leading a small white duck by a chain.
  "What can I do for you, madam?" the psychiatrist asked.
  "Oh, it's not me," said the woman, "it's my husband. He thinks he's a duck."

- Although it was only her first visit, the harried husband asked the psychiatrist if he had made any progress in treating his wife's mania for changing things. The psychiatrist stroked his chin thoughtfully and then replied, "As a matter of fact, she spent the entire time moving my couch around to see if it wouldn't look better in some other spot."

- "I must say," burbled the hostess, "I think my analyst is the best in the world! You can't imagine what he's done for me. You ought to try him."
  "But I don't need analysis," said the star. "I couldn't be more normal—there's nothing wrong with me."
  "But he's absolutely great," insisted her friend. "He'll find *something* wrong."

■ A man visited a psychiatrist and said: "Every time I step out of my apartment there's a lion waiting to jump me."

The psychiatrist gave the matter some thought and replied: "Your mind is playing tricks on you, and you need psychiatric care. I suggest you come in for consultation three times a week."

The man did as suggested and visited the psychiatrist several times, then missed a visit.

The psychiatrist phoned the patient's house and, when the wife answered the phone, the doctor asked: "How is your husband?"

"Haven't you heard?" she replied sorrowfully. "When he stepped out of the door this morning, a lion ate him up."

Psychology

■ After the college boy delivered the telegram the man at the door asked, "What is the usual tip for a delivery?"

"Well," replied the youth, "this is my first trip here, but the other fellows say that if I get a half dollar out of you, I'm doing great."

"Is that so?" snorted the man. "Just to show them how wrong they are here's a dollar."

"Thanks," replied the messenger. "I'll put this into my special school fund."

"What are you studying?" asked the man.

The lad smiled. "Applied psychology."

—*Emil Berger*

Publishing

■ The trouble with the publishing business is that too many people who have half a mind to write a book do so.

■ An old subscriber recently wrote to the editor of the British magazine *Punch* and complained: "Your magazine isn't as good as it used to be." Replied the editor: "It never was."

■ A youngster looking in a bookstore window asked his mother, "What are those things?"

"Those are books, dear. That's what the movies we see on television are made of."

R

Reference

- The Director of a Human Service Agency was called on to provide a reference for a live-in house-parent.

    "Could you describe Mary's general personality?" asked the caller.

    "She enjoys a good appetite, is cautious about her work, and has no trouble sleeping," responded the director.

    Confused by the vague response, the potential employer continued, "Well, how did you feel when Mary left your employment?"

    "Well," responded the director, "Mary worked here one year, and when she left, we were pleased."

Resourcefulness

- An industrial concern in a small city desired certain concessions in order to put into effect a program of expansion. There was the customary element of opposition, which advanced the theory that the company was of no special importance, and the city would fare as well without its presence. Thereupon the company commenced to make payment to its employees in silver dollars instead of the usual paper currency. Silver dollars began to flow over the counters in stores, into filling stations and theaters and refreshment stands. Where silver dollars had been all but forgotten legal tender, they flowed in every kind of transaction. The influence of the company was better understood, and the opposition to the expansion was withdrawn.

- A merchant was waiting to determine which of his two sons was the more worthy of inheriting his property. He gave each a coin and said: "Buy with this money something which will fill this house."

    The elder son hurried to the market place where he learned that the cheapest and bulkiest thing he could buy was straw. He spent his coin for that, but had not enough even to cover the floor.

The youngest son, perceiving that his father had entrusted him with a commission which could be executed only by unusual shrewdness, deliberated and finally spent his coin for candles. These he took home and lighted, one in each room, so that the light they gave filled the house.

"To you," said the happy father, "I give over my business. You have shown true wisdom."

Restaurant—Restaurants

- *Restaurant sign*: "Customers who find the waiters rude should see the manager."

- *Vexed diner*: "You say you're the same waiter who took my order? Somehow I expected a much older man."

- *Man in restaurant, beckoning waiter*: "Is it raining outside?"

- *Waiter*: "Sorry, sir, this isn't my table."

- There's a restaurant in Chicago which never draws a line through menu items that are sold out. Instead, they use a rubber stamp reading: "This was too good!"

- "Look here," said the annoyed diner. "How can I eat with all those girls staring at me?"

  "I'm not supposed to tell you," explained the waiter, "but part of your dinner came from the cooking school next door. If you just taste their dishes and don't eat them, those girls flunk."

- A customer in a smart restaurant complained that the lobster he had ordered had a claw missing.

  "I'm sorry, sir," said the waiter, "but our lobsters are so fresh they fight one another in the kitchen."

  "Well, take this one back and bring me one of the winners," snapped the customer.

- As the luncheon hour approached, a restaurant manager called his servers together. "Today," he said, "I want you all to look your very best. Put on a little extra makeup, see that your hair is clean, and greet each customer with a big smile."

  "What's this all about?" asked one server. "VIP's coming in today?"

  "No," sighed the manager, "the beef is tough."

- Three elderly women were stranded in a tough neighborhood at tea time, so they reluctantly stopped in at a local greasy spoon and ordered from the grizzled waiter.

  "I'll have a cup of strong tea," said one, "and no lemon."

  "Some weak tea, and lemon," said the second.

  "Tea for me, too," said the third. "But make sure the cup is clean."

  The waiter dutifully wrote down their instructions and returned in ten minutes with their orders.

  "Okay," he grumbled, "who gets the clean cup?"

S

Sales

- As President of Neiman-Marcus, Stanley Marcus trained his sales-people how to spot a potential sale: "As long as your customer is alive, you have a prospect."

- A sales manager was giving a motivational pep-talk to his sales representatives. "Each of your offices cost this company $5,000," he said.

  "Impossible," one man said. "The furniture in my office isn't worth half that much."

  "Maybe not," responded the manager, "but that's what it costs us each time you sit in your office rather than going out making contracts and creating business."

- A salesperson who covers a chair instead of their territory will always be on the bottom.

- The law of diminishing returns catches up with the salesperson who rests on their laurels.

- The cub Florida real estate salesperson asked her boss if she could refund the money to an irate customer who discovered the land he had bought was under water.

  "What kind of salesperson are you?" demanded the boss. "Go out there and sell him a motor boat."

- The colonel reviewing the troops on parade looked long and hard, frowned, and then barked at the captain: "What's the idea of parading all the big men in front of the smaller men?"

  "Sorry, sir," explained the captain, "but it seems the sergeant ran a fruit stand before he enlisted."

- The ace sales agent returned after six weeks on the road and presented his expense account to the manager. "What's this big item here on your expense account?" growled the boss.

  "Oh," replied the salesperson, "that's my hotel bill."

  "Well," grunted the boss, "don't buy any more hotels."

- A youngster walked into a bank to open an account with $25. The bank's vice president gave him a warming smile and asked him how he accumulated so much money.

  "Selling magazine subscriptions," said the lad.

  "You've done well. Sold them to lots of people, obviously."

  "Nope," answered the little boy proudly. "I sold them all to one family...their dog bit me."

- For more than six months a salesperson had been calling on the buyer of a certain firm, but the buyer never bought anything. After each interview the salesperson would say, "Thank you very much. I wish I had fifty customers like you."

  Mystified, the buyer finally said, "Look here, I don't mind your coming in here every week or two and showing your samples. I buy nothing, but you always say the same thing—'Thank you very much. I wish I had fifty customers like you.' Why do you make this statement?"

  "Well," replied the salesperson, smiling, "right now I have about two hundred customers like you. I really do wish that I had only fifty."

- When a man wrote to an insurance company asking for some information, he added a warning note saying, "I don't want any advertising material—and no salesperson." It was difficult to put the information into a letter, so the company ignored the letter and its warning and sent a salesperson around to see the man anyway. The fellow didn't wait for an explanation. "I told them," he said "no salesperson!"

The caller—a youngster just out of the insurance company's training school—sighed and replied, "Mister, I'm as close to no-salesperson as they've got."

- A small businessperson was in trouble with her sales. She decided to call in an expert to give her an outsider's viewpoint.

  After he had gone over her plans and problems, the businessperson took the sales expert to a map on the wall and showed him brightly colored pins stuck wherever she had a salesperson. Looking at the expert, she asked, "Now for a starter, what is the first thing we should do?"

  "Well," replied the expert, "the first thing is to take those pins out of the map and stick them into the salespeople."

- The sales manager of a large firm was always trying to get the salespeople to think for themselves.

  One day he received a telegram from one of his people who was en route to Salt Lake City. It read: "Have lost order pads. Shall I proceed to destination or return to the office?"

  The sales manager wired back: "Yes."

  Within an hour, another message arrived from the bewildered salesperson: "Do you mean yes I should proceed to destination or yes I should return to the office?"

  Whereupon the sales manager sent this laconic telegram: "No."

- The sporting enthusiast went to a hunting lodge and bagged a record number of birds with the help of a dog named "Seller."

  The following year the man wrote the lodge again for reservations requesting the same dog, "Seller."

  As soon as he arrived at the lodge he asked the handler if "Seller" was ready to hunt.

  "Hound ain't no durn good now," the handler said.

  "What happened," cried the man, "was he injured?"

  "Nope! Some fool came down here and called him 'Sales Manager' all week. Now all he does is sit on his tail and bark."

Secretary—Secretaries

- The first thing a new secretary types is the boss.

- Before arguing with the boss, it's well to look at both sides: their side and the outside.

- The secretary was telling her friends about her latest squabble with the boss. "All I asked her was 'Do you want the carbon copy double spaced, too?'"

- The boss wasn't sure how to take it when her efficient secretary handed her a batch of letters and said, "One of them is marked 'personal' but it really isn't."

- A minister's new secretary, who had formerly worked at the Pentagon, set about reorganizing the minister's filing system. She labeled one drawer "sacred" and the other "top sacred."

- Told that her teen-age daughter was having difficulty with reading and writing, her mother appeared unconcerned.

- "It really doesn't matter," she said, "she'll always have a secretary."

- A busy school superintendent told his secretary that he would be very busy during the afternoon and didn't want to see any callers. "If they say their business is important, just tell them 'That's what they all say.'"
  During the afternoon a lady called and insisted on seeing the superintendent. Finally she explained, "I am his wife."
  The secretary smilingly replied, "That's what they all say."

Size

- A customer goes into a pet store and points to a large dog and asks: "How much?"
  The proprietor says, "$50."
  The guy points to a medium-size dog and asks: "And how much is that one?"
  "$100," replies the pet store owner.
  "Well," the guy persists, "how much is that little teeny weeny dog in the corner?"
  "That one is $200," the proprietor says.
  The guy gets an alarmed look on his face. "How much will it cost me if I don't buy any dog at all?"
  —Ollie M. James

Statistics

- It has now been proven beyond a doubt that smoking is the major cause of statistics.

- She was reading birth and death statistics. Suddenly she turned to a man near her and said, "Do you know that every time I breathe a man dies?"

  "Very interesting," he returned, "have you tried toothpaste?"

- Checking some questionnaires that had just been filled in, a census clerk was amazed to note that one of them contained figures 121 and 125 in the spaces for "Age of Mother, If Living" and "Age of Father, If Living."

  "Surely your parents can't be as old as this?" asked the incredulous clerk.

  "Well, no," was the answer, "but they would be, if living."

Subtlety

- A prominent minister was asked to give his opinion of advertising in the United States. He hesitated to make any comment on advertising but he did offer to pray for the people who make a living at it.

Success

- Soft words sung in a lullaby will put a babe to sleep. Excited words will stir a mob to violence. Eloquent words will send armies marching into the face of death. Encouraging words will fan to flame the genius of a Rembrandt or a Lincoln. Powerful words will mold the public mind as the sculptor molds his clay. Words, spoken or written, are a dynamic force.

  Writing of Napoleon and his Italian campaign, Emil Ludwig said:

  "Half of what he achieves is achieved by the power of words."

  Words are the swords we use in our battle for success and happiness. How others react towards us depends, in a large measure, upon the words we speak to them. Life is a great whispering gallery that sends back echoes of the words we send out! Our words are immortal, too. They go marching through the years in the lives of all those with whom we come in contact.

When you speak, when you write, remember the creative power of words.

—*Wilfred Peterson*

- Robert A. Beck, chairman emeritus of the Prudential Insurance Company of America, shared these thoughts on success in a speech he delivered to the Wall Street Seminar:

  Beat yesterday: "Always produce more than you did the day before."

  Success is never an accident: "Every good record is built with defined goals and a realistic strategy. It doesn't just happen."

  Be a good example: "You don't have to be an extrovert, but you should look like a positive force in the way you walk, dress, and meet colleagues."

  Get involved: "Reach out for new opportunities; be involved in industry matters, not just in your own company."

  Make your career fun: "Once you master a task you don't like, it's easier and also a source of pride and accomplishment."

  Let the music out: "Too many people live and die with the music still in them. Be fully committed; then you will achieve your goals."

  Success is easier than failure: "Working hard is not difficult as long as you get the results you want. It's easier to live with yourself when you can be proud of what you've done."

T

Tact

- Tact is the art of making guests feel at home when that's really where you wish they were.

—*George E. Bergman*

Taxes

- Today's dime is really a dollar with the taxes taken out.

- A dog's life can't be too bad; someone else pays his taxes.

- One difference between death and taxes is that death doesn't get worse every time Congress meets.

- It's getting so that children will have to be educated to realize that "damn" and "taxes" are two separate words.

- A man used to pay a luxury tax on his billfold, an income tax on the stuff he put into it, and a sales tax whenever he took anything out.

- Folks used to worry because they couldn't take it with them. In today's tax climate their only worry is whether it will last as long as they do.

Technique

- "How can you possibly tell the weather with a piece of rope?" the tourist wanted to know.

  "It's simple, sonny," was the droll answer. "When the rope swings back and forth, it's windy, and when it gits wet, it's raining."

- Fascinated by the dispatch with which the youngest mother on the block got rid of pesky salespeople, a neighbor asked for the secret.

  "Oh, it's very simple," the girl smiled. "I tell them I'm so glad they've come because I want to show them my latest line of greeting cards."

- A man stood on the street corner waiting to cross while the traffic streamed by, swift and continuous. After a very long wait, the man became impatient, but he dared not risk going out into the traffic. He spied another man on the other side of the street and called out to him: "Hey, I say, how did you get over there?"

  The other man cupped his hands around his mouth and shouted: "I was born over here!"

Trade Mark

- "Why do you have an apple for your trade mark?" asked a client of his tailor.

  "Well," replied the tailor, rubbing his hands, "if it hadn't been for an apple, where would the clothing business be today?"

Travel

- Those who say you can't take it with you never saw a car packed for a vacation trip.

- Two Spanish children, aged four and six, were turning over the pages of an art book. "Look!" one of them suddenly cried, pointing to some Rubens nudes: "Tourists! Tourists!"

- Two Boston ladies were sightseeing in California on a very warm day. "It never gets like this in Boston," remarked one, fanning herself rapidly.

  "Of course not," returned the other. "But you have to remember that here we are 3,000 miles from the ocean."

- A couple finally realized a lifelong ambition by spending a vacation in Europe. Upon their return they were interviewed by a reporter for the local newspaper.

  "And did you see much poverty abroad?" he inquired.

  "See it!" snorted the husband, "I brought some of it back with me."

Twins

- Mrs. Brown struck up a conversation with the small son of her new neighbor.

  "I understand," she said, "that you have two sets of twins at your house. That's wonderful! Are you one of the twins?"

  "No, ma'am," was the gloomy response, "I'm just a spare."

U

Understanding

- Napoleon Bonaparte was a stickler for crystal clear communications. He had a saying that applies to much of today's world of business: "An order that can be misunderstood, will be misunderstood." The story goes that Napoleon kept an idiot sitting on a camp chair outside his headquarters. The idiot wore corporal's stripes because he served a very important purpose. Whenever

Napoleon wrote an order, he would show it first to the idiot. If the idiot understood the order, Napoleon felt it was safe to transmit it.

- Albert Einstein struggled to get people to understand his theory of relativity. This important, yet complicated discovery was met with skepticism. One day Einstein was asked to explain his theory "in terms anyone could understand." He calmly answered, "If you sit with a pretty girl for an hour, it seems like a minute. If you sit on a hot stove for a minute, it seems much longer than any hour. That's relativity!"

- Two business retailers were discussing the difficulties of their trade. "I can't remember business ever being this bad," Joe commented. "My April sales were the worst I've seen in several years. Then June came along. What a disaster. And, July was even worse."

  "You haven't seen anything," groaned his friend. "My son dropped out of college and joined a commune. My teenage daughter told me yesterday she was pregnant and plans to drop out of high school. And now my marriage partner for the last twenty-three years tells me there is no love left in our relationship. It doesn't get any worse than this."

  "Oh yes it does," replied Joe. "My August sales."

V

Vacation—Vacations

- The bigger the summer vacation...the harder the fall.

- Nobody needs a vacation so badly as those who just had one.

- The alternative to a vacation is to stay home and tip every third person you see.

- Put some money away for a rainy day and it's a safe bet you'll spend it on your holiday.

- When some people say they are saving up for a summer vacation, some mean the next, others the last one.

- The sum of the parts can be greater than the whole—as people find out when they start repacking that vacation suitcase.

- Vacation is a wonderful time. After a couple of weeks of it you feel good enough to go back to work and so poor you have to.

- A vacation should be just long enough for the boss to miss you, and not long enough for him to discover how well he can get along without you.

- *New employee*: "Do you give your clerks two weeks vacation?"

- *Boss*: "No, they get a month—two weeks when I go on my vacation and two weeks when they go on theirs."

- "Mummy," said the little boy, "why does the minister get a month's holiday in the summer when Daddy only gets two weeks?"

  "Well, son," answered Mother, "if he is a good minister, he needs it. If he isn't, the congregation needs it!"

- An efficiency expert went in to see the boss about his vacation. He came out with a dejected expression on his face.

  Asked what was wrong, he replied: "I got only one week. The boss says I'm so efficient I can have as much fun in one week as other people can in two."

Value—Values

- Mahatma Ghandi once wrote that there were seven sins in the world: wealth without work, pleasure without conscience, knowledge without character, commerce without morality, science without humanity, worship without sacrifice, politics without principle.

- "It's easy to have principles when you're rich," said Ray Kroc, the McDonald's hamburger magnate. "The important thing is to have principles when you are poor."

  When Ray Kroc opened his first restaurant in Des Plaines, Illinois, on Friday, April 15, 1955, the ending receipts on the cash register that day totaled $366.12. Within two weeks, sales doubled. In 1987, the McDonalds restaurants grossed more than $14.3 billion.

McDonalds' executives attribute their success to a devotion to their corporate values, established by Ray Kroc before he was rich. Their standards of excellence stem from the values of "quality, service, cleanliness, and value."

■ It is said that about 200 years ago, the tomb of the great conqueror Charlemagne was opened. The sight the workmen saw was startling. There was his body in a sitting position, clothed in the most elaborate of kingly garments, with a scepter in his bony hand. On his knee lay a New Testament, with a cold, lifeless finger pointing to *Mark 8:36*: "For what shall it profit a man, if he shall gain the whole world, and lose his own soul?"

W

Wages

■ A farmer, in great need of extra hands at haying time, finally asked Si Warren, a town character, if he could help out.

"What'll ye pay?" asked Si.

"I'll pay what you're worth," replied the farmer.

Si scratched his head a minute, then said, "I won't work for that!"

■ One of the neatest ways of asking the boss for a raise was the approach used by John Kieran when he was the sports columnist of the *New York Times*. Feeling the need for more dough but wanting to be tactful about it, Kieran went to his employer, Adolph Ochs, and said respectfully, "Mr. Ochs, working for the *Times* is a luxury I can no longer afford."

He got the raise.

■ MacSweeney, the carpenter, had just been granted another raise in pay but when his brother from the country asked him how he was getting along, he sighed and sadly shook his head. "But you've got a good job, haven't you?" asked his brother.

"One of the best," replied MacSweeney.

"What's the trouble, then?"

"The wages—that's the trouble."

"But I thought you just had a big raise in pay."

"By golly, that's just what's bothering me. My wages are so dab-blamed high now I can't ever afford to take a day off."

Warning

■ A woman stopped at a small town garage and told the mechanic, "Whenever I hit eighty, there's a terrible knocking in the engine."

The mechanic gave the vehicle a prolonged and thorough examination, and after much testing, wiped the grease from his hands and drawled, "I don't see nothin' wrong. It must be the good Lord a'warnin' you."

Wealth

■ He started as poor as the proverbial church mouse twenty years ago. He has now retired with a fortune of $500,000. This money was acquired through economy, conscientious effort to give full value, indomitable perseverance, and the death of an uncle who left him $499,000.

■ "I'm glad to find you as you are," said the old friend. "Your wealth hasn't changed you."

"Well," replied the candid millionaire, "it has changed me in one way. I am now eccentric where I used to be impolite, and delightfully witty where I used to be rude."

■ The world might have never heard of Voltaire as a writer if he hadn't been a math whiz. Taking advantage of a government miscalculation in issuing a national lottery, he formed a syndicate and bought up every ticket. His share made him independent and gave him time to write. His success was assured by the Paris censors, who always banned his books and closed his plays.

■ To show their contempt for wealth ("Who steals my gold steals trash"), the original owners of the Venetian Palazzo Rezzonico, after giving great banquets, used to throw the gold plate into the side canal. However, a net had first been placed in the canal and, after the departure of all the guests, it was hauled in and the gold plate replaced in its repository.

- Years ago, when Ernie Pyle was on the *Washington News* as a $30-a-week copyreader, he tagged a story with the headline: "Man Inherits Huge Fortune of $15,000."

  "Where did you get the idea that $15,000 is a huge fortune?" his executive editor asked.

  "If you were earning the same dough I am," Ernie replied, "you'd think so, too."

- A certain member of the nobility had a valet who was violently opposed to the capitalistic system, and who devoted most of his spare time to attending meetings where he could listen while communistic theories were expounded. The master was tolerant because the servant was diligent in the performance of his duties. Suddenly the valet stopped going to meetings, and after several weeks the master became curious enough to ask the reason.

  "At the last meeting I attended," said the valet, "it was proved that if all the wealth in the country were divided equally among all the people, the share of each person would be two thousand francs."

  "So what?" asked the master.

  "Well, I have five thousand francs."

- One day a farmer came to pay his rent to a man whose love of money was very great. After settling the account, the farmer said, "I will give you a quarter if you will let me go down to your vault and look at your money."

  The farmer was permitted to see the piles of gold and silver in the miser's big chest. After gazing for a while the farmer said, "Now I am as well off as you are."

  "How can that be?" asked the hoarder.

  "Why, sir," said the farmer, "you never use any of this money. All you do with it is look at it. I have looked at it, too, so I am just as rich as you are."

Witness—Witnesses

- "Judge, I don't know what to do."

  "Why, what's wrong?"

  "Well, I swore to tell the truth, but every time I try, some lawyer objects."

■ "You seem to have plenty of intelligence for a man in your position," sneered the attorney to the man on the witness stand.

"Thank you," answered the witness. "If I weren't under oath, I'd return the compliment."

■ The attorney demanded severely, "You can testify that you saw the defendant strike the complaining witness, and yet you were three blocks away. Just how far can you see, anyhow?"

"Oh, I don't know exactly," the witness drawled, "about a million miles, I expect—just how far away is the moon?"

■ "Mr. Witness, you're not telling the same story now that you did right after the shooting happened, are you?"

"No, sir."

"Well, how do you explain the difference?"

"Well," replied the witness, "I was talkin' then; I'm swearin' now."

■ A man was on trial for an offense, and his sanity was being questioned.

"Have you ever noticed if the accused was in the habit of talking to himself when he was alone?"

"I have no idea."

"No idea! But surely you are his closest friend?"

"Yes, but I was never with him when he was alone."

■ A lawyer was browbeating a witness. "I understand," he snarled, "that you called on the defendant. What did he say to you at that time?"

Counsel for the other side objected that an answer would be hearsay and not admissible. The first lawyer contended that direct testimony as to what was said did not constitute hearsay. A long argument followed. The judge retired to chambers to consider the point. He returned after some time to rule that the question was a proper one.

"Now," continued the lawyer triumphantly, "what did the defendant tell you when you called on him?"

"Nothing, sir. He wasn't home," was the meek reply.

■ An elderly mountaineer on the witness stand was cool as a cucumber. The prosecuting attorney grew impatient.

"Do you swear that this is not your signature?"

"Yep."

"It is not your handwriting?"

"Nope."

"Does it resemble your handwriting?"

"Nope...can't say it does at all."

"Do you swear it doesn't resemble your handwriting in a single particular?"

"I certainly do."

"How can you be so certain about it?"

Swiftly the witness replied, "Can't write."

■ Jim Murphy had been accused of selling liquor illicitly and the prosecuting attorney was endeavoring to make Pat, a job teamster, admit that he had delivered liquor to the defendant. He stated that he had once delivered freight to Murphy and that part of that freight was a barrel, but when asked what the barrel contained he replied that he didn't know.

"Don't know! Wasn't the barrel marked?" asked the attorney.

"Yes, sir."

"Then how dare you tell the court that you don't know what was in it?"

"Because, sir, the barrel was marked 'Jim Murphy' on one end and 'Bourbon Whiskey' on the other. How the devil was I to know which was in it?"

■ A witness was being examined as to his knowledge of a shooting affair.

"Did you see the shot fired?" the magistrate asked.

"No, sir, I only heard it," was the evasive reply.

"The evidence is not satisfactory," replied the magistrate sternly. "Stand down!"

The witness turned around to leave the box and as soon as his back was turned he laughed derisively.

The magistrate, indignant at his contempt of court, called him back and asked him how he dared to laugh in court.

Queried the offender, "Did you see me laugh, Your Honor?"

■ An extremely obstreperous woman was in the witness chair in a case in court. "I want a chance to tell this story in my own way," she declared. "I want to tell it exactly as it happened and without being interrupted at every other word by that lousy, sarcastic shyster over there who..."

"Just a moment, madam," said the judge sternly. "You cannot use that kind of language in this courtroom. What you mean is 'the counsel for the defense.' Now start your testimony over again."

"All right," sighed the witness. "As I was saying, I want to tell this story in my own way—exactly how it happened without being interrupted at every other word by that—" She broke off suddenly, turned to the judge and said: "Your Honor, what was that fancy name you called that lousy, sarcastic shyster?"

Woman—Women

■ At a large banquet, Lady Astor once remarked that men are more vain than women and, meeting with stormy opposition, declared herself ready to substantiate her statement. Steering the conversation to men's fashions, she suddenly said in a loud voice: "It's a pity that the most intelligent and learned men attach least importance to the way they dress. Why, right at this table the most cultivated man is wearing the most clumsily knotted tie!"

As if on a given signal, every man in the room immediately put his hand to his tie to straighten it.

Work

■ The patient explained to the doctor that he was unable to perform all the responsibilities of his job that he used to. The doctor ran a series of tests and questioned the patient for further details. When the examination was complete, the curious patient said, "Tell it to me straight, doctor. I can handle the results."

"Well, it is quite simple," the doctor replied, "you're just plain lazy."

"Okay, I can take that," said the man. "Now could you write down the medical term so I can give it to my supervisor?"

■ I am wondering what would have happened to me if some fluent talker had converted me to the theory of the eight-hour day and convinced me that it was not fair to my fellow workers to put forth my best efforts in my work. I am glad that the eight-hour day had not been invented when I was a young man. If my life had been made up of eight-hour days I do not believe I could have accomplished a great deal. This country would not amount to as much as it does if the young men of fifty years ago had been afraid that they might earn more than they were paid for.

—*Thomas A. Edison*

- "Work does more to dignify the individual than high office or public praise!" declared John Ruskin, the English critic. "Young men and women who learn to respect work, and who enter into it with eagerness and abandon, will reach maturity with a solid foundation for happy and useful living."

  Work is a tonic that tones the system for play.

  Work is not only a way to make a living, it is the way to make a life.

  If "all work and no play makes Jack a dull boy," then all play and no work makes Jack a dangerous boy.

  Work with the hands can only result from work with the brain, for the brain is the master of the hands.

  Work is not merely a means to an end, it is an end in itself. Blessed is he who loves his work, for he shall know great joy from day to day.

- Kemmons Wilson, the founder of Holiday Inns, is a phenomenal success story. He never graduated from high school yet spearheaded the successful development of Holiday Inn. Ironically, yet understandably, he was asked to give the commencement address for a graduating class at the high school he attended. He said, "I'm not sure why I'm here. I never got a degree, and I've only worked half days my entire life. My advice to you is to do the same. Work half days every day. And it doesn't matter which half...the first twelve hours or the second twelve hours."

Y

Youth

- On an NBC television broadcast, Lewis B. Hershey, as Draft Director was discussing the question of when a boy becomes an adult.

"A boy becomes an adult," he said, "three years before his parents think he does—and about two years after he thinks he does."

■ A child asked a man to pick a flower for her. That was simple enough. But when she said, "Now put it back," the man experienced a baffling helplessness he never knew before. "How can you explain that it cannot be done?" he asked. "How can one make clear to young people that there are some things which when once broken, once mutilated, can never be replaced or mended?"